TIMES TO REMEMBER

© Copyright 1988, 2025 John Kropp. All rights reserved.
ISBN Softcover 978-0-646-70496-8
Second edition (with added photographs)

No portion of this book may be reproduced, stored in a retrieval system or transmitted in any form or by any means—electronic, mechanical, photocopy, recording or otherwise—except for brief quotations in printed reviews or promotion, without prior written permission from the author.

Front cover photo: From the Beacon, looking towards Imbil.
All photos used with permission.

Typeset in Minion, Yeseva One and Raleway

Cataloguing in Publishing Data
Title: Times to Remember
Author: John Kropp
Subjects: Historical non-fiction; memoir; geography

A copy of this title is held at the National Library of Australia.

Times to Remember

HISTORY FROM YABBA, BELLA, LITTLE BELLA AND KINGAHAM CREEK RESIDENTS.

JOHN KROPP

CONTENTS

FOREWORD	1
HOW THEY WERE NAMED	2
BELLA JUNCTION STATE SCHOOL TEACHERS	3
BELLA JUNCTION STATE SCHOOL	4
REGISTER OF PUPILS BELLA JUNCTION SCHOOL	12
GOLD MINING	20
TIMBER	21
DAIRYING	25
STIRLING'S CROSSING	28
YABBA CREEK SLEEPER MILL	30
GLENVEAGH – VIA IMBIL	32
GLENVEAGH – BELLA CREEK ROAD, VIA IMBIL	34
MANTHEY'S PROPERTY	36
PORTION 70 – PARISH IMBIL	38
ATTHOW FAMILY	42
ATTHOW FAMILY	44
THE ANGUS HERD (THREE GENERATIONS)	47
PORTION 7 PARISH IMBIL – DEEP CREEK CROSSING, YABBA CREEK	50

BILLY FRIENDS' FARM PORTION 12 PARISH IMBIL – COUNTY LENNOX	52
PORTION 12, PARISH IMBIL – COUNTY LENNOX	54
SUB 2 PORTION 870 – PARISH BROOLOO	56
SMALL RECOLLECTIONS	58
SUB 2 PORTION 870 – PARISH BROOLOO	59
ANDREASSEN – PORTION 168043 LOT 1 – PARISH BROOLOO	63
ANDREASSEN – BUTLERS CORNER	64
SUB 4 PORTION 870 – PARISH BROOLOO	65
PORTION 438 – PARISH OF IMBIL	69
RECREATION	71
MEMORIES – TIMBER	72
MEMORIES – OTHER	73
PORTION 438, PARISH IMBIL, COUNTY LENNOX SHIRE WIDGEE	75
ROBSON FAMILY	77
"ENROH" – YABBA CREEK	79
GEORGE GARRETT FAMILY (1884-1967)	81
PORTION 34 PARISH IMBIL LIFE ON A DAIRY FARM AT BUTLER'S CORNER	87
NEUCOM'S PROPERTY	90
PORTION 100V – PARISH BROOLOO	97

PORTION 25V – PARISH IMBIL	99
MRS. M DWYER RECOLLECTS	101
REX TWEED REMEMBERS	102
LIFE ON YABBA CREEK FARM MID-TWENTIES TO FORTIES	103
LIFE ON A FARM	107
QLD COUNTRY LIFE, OCTOBER 6, 1983	110
REMINISCENCE	112
MEMORIES - FIRST PLANE	115
PLEASURES AND PERILS OF SCHOOL DAYS	116
MEMORIES - FIRST CAR	118
MEMORIES - FIRST WIRELESS	120
MEMORIES - THE GOLDEN SOVEREIGNS	121
MEMORIES - "BLACK WHISKERS" OR "THE HAIRY MAN"	122
LOVELY – OUR PET DEER	123
QUEENSLAND WATER RESOURCES COMMISSION BORUMBA DAM	127
WELCOME TO LAKE BORUMBA FISH HATCHERY	128
BRISBANE GIRLS GRAMMAR SCHOOL	130

FOREWORD

So often, as we live in a familiar environment for a period of time, we tend to allow events in our lives to pass us by. History is not only a written record of the past but also a statement of events that happen at the present time, so that what is recorded now, will in time become the history for future generations.

This book has recorded events of those people who live and have lived on the upper reaches of Yabba Creek.

Dramatic changes have taken place in the area since the turn of the century, and this is revealed in the articles written in this book.

I would like to take this opportunity to thank those people who have given time and effort to write and who gave information for this book.

John Kropp
Reunion Coordinator for properties west of Imbil along Yabba Creek, Bella Creek, Little Bella Creek, & Kingaham Creek

HOW THEY WERE NAMED

BORUMBA (CREEK)

"Place of Minnows" from the Kabi word "burun", the name of the mountain minnow (Galaxias), also called common jollytail or eel-gudgeon. "Ba" is usually rendered in English as "Place of".

IMBIL

Aboriginal word for a scrub vine. Mr. McTaggart, a highly respected colonist who was born in Campbelltown, Argyle, Scotland in November 1823, held the following pastoral blocks on the western side of the Mary River in the 1850s – Cordalba, Bunya Creek and Bluff Plain. He died at Kilkivan on 16.1.1871. Bunya Creek and Bluff Plain were consolidated to form Imbil holding, which was leased by Clement and Paul Lawless on 1.1.1869.

The town of Imbil was a result of the subdivision of part of the holding in 1914.

KINGAHAM (CREEK)

Meaning is not given in the Queensland Place Names record.

YABBA (CREEK)

A corruption of "Yapper", a currajong tree. Yabba run was held by Alexander Swanson at the time of the Gympie gold rush (1867).

BELLA (CREEK)

Supposition named after Aboriginal Chief's Lubra "Bella Bella". No record of this could be found but this is the meaning adopted by most locals.

BELLA JUNCTION STATE SCHOOL TEACHERS

McKee, Norah	28.03.28 - 03.09.28
O'Leary, Honorah	03.09.28 - 18.08.30
Kemp, Elsie	25.08.30 - 07.02.32
Middleton, Ivor Graham	22.02.32 - 11.07.32

School closed 10.07.32

BELLA JUNCTION STATE SCHOOL

Year	Average Attendance
1928	11.3
1929	12.61
1930	11.1
1931	10.15
1932	8.4

Christmas break-up 1928
Back: T.Schellbach, J.Friend, B.Atthow, M.Saunders, W.Boardman, E.Ford, H.Atthow nursing D.Friend. Middle: (Pupils) B.Schellbach, W.Schellbach, B.Boardman, E.Saunders, J.Schellbach, M.Boardman, M.Schellbach, L.Schellbach, R.Atthow.
Front: G Boardman, S.Atthow, E.Boardman, D.Friend, D.Saunders.

Bella Junction
1410

Report on Accommodation for Teachers.

14460/29

Name of School __Bella Junction__   No. of School __1410__

Situation of School __Seven miles from Imbil__

Date of Inspection __17.6.29__   Inspector __K.A. Somers__

Finished 10.7.29

Whether accommodation is available for
- (a) Female __Yes__
- (b) Male __Yes__

Whether more than one householder offers accommodation for
- (a) Female __No__
- (b) Male __No__

Householders Offering Accommodation for Teachers.

NAMES.	FEMALE TEACHER.		MALE TEACHER.	
	Distance from School.	Approximate Cost Weekly.	Distance from School.	Approximate Cost Weekly.
Mrs. J. Donald	3 mls	25/-	3 mls	30/-

Remarks: The teacher rides daily and has to cross Yabba Creek three times. The horse is provided by Mr. Donald; the teacher has her own saddle and bridle. It is quite impossible to reach the school during heavy rain. There is no suitable accommodation nearer. Conditions at Mrs. McDonald's are satisfactory.

(Signed) K.A. Somers
District Inspector.

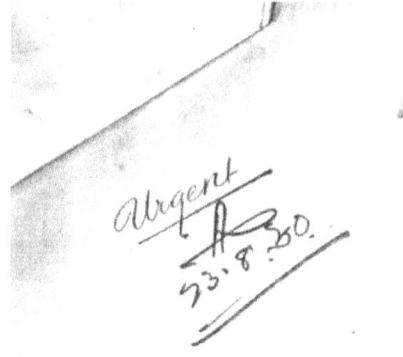

1410.
Bella Junction
J. E. Schellback

Urgent
23.8.30.

No teacher attending school.

RECEIVED TELEGRAM

STATION FROM: IMBIL   WORDS: 14

42727   To 19 AUG 1930   UNDER SECRETARY EDUCATION
DEPARTMENT BRISBANE

NO TEACHER ATTENDING BELLA JUNCTION SCHOOL WAITING EXPLANATION

SCHELLBACK

2 27pm sg

19 AUG 1930

1. On the 19th instant sender was advised of the transfer of Miss R. Kemp, from the State School at Hodgsons Vale, to the Provisional School at Bella Junction, as from the date of her entry on duty therein.

2. Acknowledging receipt of this telegram refer writer to Departmental communication of the 19th instant.

3. It is worthy of note that a "RUSH" paper which left this Branch on the 12th instant did not reach the Correspondence Branch until the 19th idem Ordinary correspondence could hardly proceed more slowly.

22.8.30

TIMES TO REMEMBER

QUEENSLAND STATE ARCHIVES

Department of Education:

Schools Primary

School admission registers

No: Bella Junction 1410

28 May 1928 – 8 Sep 1931

Class No: EDU/AA 62

Accession No: 413/62

S.M.S.
Dental 1.

This form is the property of and must be returned to th in fully by the parent or guar strictly as confidential.

Queer
Department of E

....School.,

TO THE PARENT OR GUARDIAN OF

(DATE)

Under arrangements which have been made in connection with the extension of the system of School Dental Inspection, provision is made for free treatment by the Dental Inspector of children under eight years of age on January 1st of the present year and children who were eligible and were treated previously, also special cases which may be brought under the notice of the Dental Inspector during the time of his visit, provided that—

> The parent's income does not exceed the basic wage or £40 per annum per member of family.

Please state whether your child is eligible for dental treatment and whether you wish or do not wish him or her to be dentally treated at all times when the Dental Inspector visits the school. If treatment is to be available, the claim for same must first be made when a child is under eight years of age.

If not living within reasonable access of a practising dentist, treatment may be claimed for all children under the age limit, regardless of the parent's income.

(Signature) ....
Head Teacher.

TO THE HEAD TEACHER,

....School.

According to the above provisions my child .... (Name in full)
is / is not entitled to receive free dental treatment and I wish / do not wish to be dentally treated at all times when the Dental Inspector visits the school.

(Signature of Parent or Guardian) ....

(Date) ....

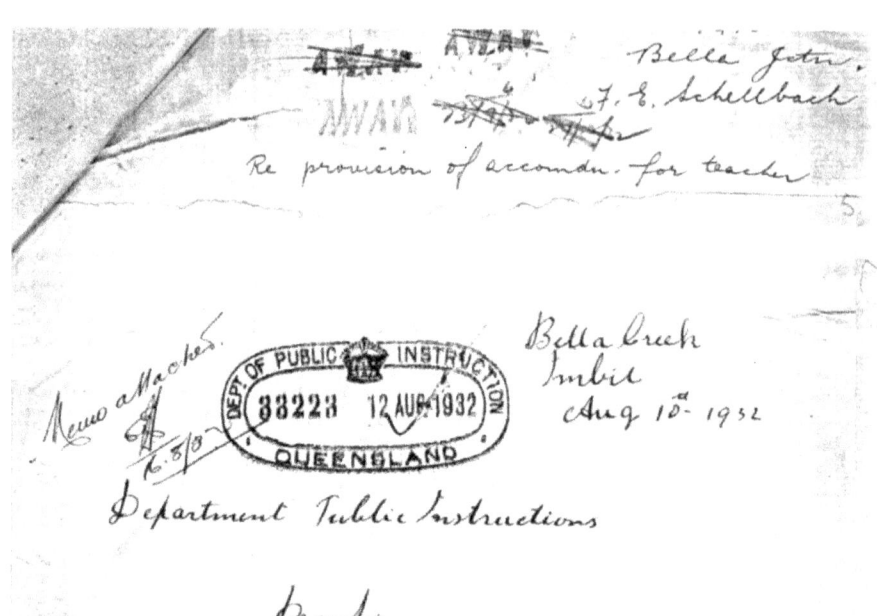

Bella John
F. E. Schellbach
Re provision of accomdn. for teacher

Bella Creek
Imbil
Aug 10th 1932

Department Public Instructions

Dear Sir

In the Event of us getting more Children for our School & getting it Re Opened; if there is No Accomodation for the Teacher to Board Would it Be Sufficient Accomodation if the School Comittee Built Two Rooms on the Back of the School. For the Teacher.

I Remain
Yours

F E Schellbach
Secretary to School Comittee

18th August, 1932

Dear Mr. Clayton,

With reference to the letter addressed to you on the 5th instant by Mr. A.H. Boardman, of Bella Junction, I wish to say that instruction by correspondence is open to all primary school pupils whose homes are more than three miles distant from the nearest school.

Circumstances do not warrant the re-opening of the Bella Junction School at the present juncture.

Yours faithfully,
B. McKenna
Director of Education

E.H.C. Clayton, Esq. M.L.A.
Parliament House,
Brisbane.

ES.
No.32/33223 Bella Junction

22nd August, 1932

Mr. F.E. Schellbach
Secretary to the School Committee,
BELLA JUNCTION, Imbil

Acknowledging the receipt of your letter of the 10th instant, I have to request you to be good enough to advise this Office whether, should the number of pupils available warrant the re-opening of the Provisional School at Bella Junction, the rooms referred to therein would be furnished adequately without cost to the Department and whether meals would be provided for the teacher. Please also to state the distance between the school and the nearest occupied residence.

Upon receipt of the information asked for the matter will receive further consideration.

B. McKenna
Director of Education

WH.
No.32/44815 Bella Junction

9th November,1932

Mr. F.E. Schellbach,
Secretary to the School Committee, B
ELLA JUNCTION, Imbil

Acknowledging the receipt of your letter of the 29th ultimo, I have to inform you that the accommodation for a teacher, particulars of which are outlined therein, would not be regarded as suitable.

You are advised that, as the prospective attendance is not sufficient, it is not intended, at present, to re-open the Provisional School at Bella Junction.

B. McKenna
Director of Education

Kids riding to school – Elbow Crossing Bridge

REGISTER OF PUPILS BELLA JUNCTION SCHOOL

Date of Admission	Pupil's Name
28.05.28	BOARDMAN, William Henry
28.05.28	BOARDMAN, Winifred May
28.05.28	BOARDMAN, Edna Mary
28.05.28	SAUNDERS, Ethel
28.05.28	SAUNDERS, Vera
28.05.28	SAUNDERS, Dorothy
28.05.28	ATTHOW, Raymond
28.05.28	ATTHOW, Shirley
28.05.28	SCHELLBACH, Evelyn Bertha
28.05.28	SCHELLBACH, William Edward
28.05.28	SCHELLBACH, Wilfred Leslie
28.05.28	SCHELLBACH, Joyce Lillian
28.05.28	SCHELLBACH, Mavis Jean
12.11.28	WALKER, Arthur
28.11.28	WALKER, Thomas
28.01.29	FRIEND, Dorothy
09.04.29	BOARDMAN, Gwendolen Rae
25.08.30	DONALD, Noel
07.07.31	SCHELLBACH, Roy
08.09.31	BOARDMAN, Nancy Ellen

School Closed on 11.07.32

TIMES TO REMEMBER

Bella Junction School building
Teacher Miss O'Leary and pupils 1930

Christmas break-up at the school

Horse-drawn Mouldboard Plough

Horse-drawn Scuffler

Pack Saddle

Sulky

Buggy

Hurricane Lamp on anvil

Hut at the Borgan

Dairy shed to store cream

Plunge dip under construction, dug by pick and shovel

Plunge dip completed

GOLD MINING

To find that larger gold nugget under this sunburnt earth has been the dream of most people. The fever that caught many a man throughout our history has also left its marks on the upper reaches of Yabba Creek.

Different people over the past have taken out mining leases and toiled day after day in the hope of finding their rainbow. One shaft dug in the 1930's by Walter Veitch using the old method of pick and shovel plus the odd stick of explosive, goes down 90 feet from the surface. The materials from the mine were loaded onto a sleigh drawn by a horse and taken to the bottom of the hill where a stamper awaited to crush the rock. This mine was closed down in the late 40's and Mr. Veitch died in 1954.

Due to the high price of gold on the world market in later years, the old mine was re-opened in 1981 by Mr. P. Tramacchi and Mr. R. Ward. The mine was called Platypus because of the number of platypuses in the waterhole adjacent to the lease. Underground mining is the method used to remove the material. The rock is then taken to Gympie to be processed.

Although gold mining has not been a large industry in the area, there will always remain the hope that the next dig will be the difference between rags and riches.

John Kropp

TIMBER

The timber located on the upper reaches of Yabba Creek and its tributaries played an important role in the development of the area and the township of Imbil. People came from near and far to buy blocks of land just for the stands of timber on them.

The cutters would set up a camp not far from the block of timber to be cut. The most popular type of camp was an iron roof with hessian walls. The advantages of this type of hut were good ventilation and you lived with, and close to nature.

With the face of the axe shining in the sun and the teeth of the cross-cut saw set to carve through the timber, men set to work falling the trees. "TIMBER!" was the call from the cutters as the trees creaked and slowly but surely fell to the ground. Another noise familiar in the scrubs in those days was that of the bullocky and his whip. He called his bullocks by name and used a few choice words in between to get his message across. Without a word in retaliation and obeying their master, the bullocks pulled in the chains and snug the logs from the scrub to the loading ramp.

With the logs loaded onto the wagons, the bullocky, calling first to his leading bullock, hauled the timber down the bush track to the sawmill or railway station at Imbil.

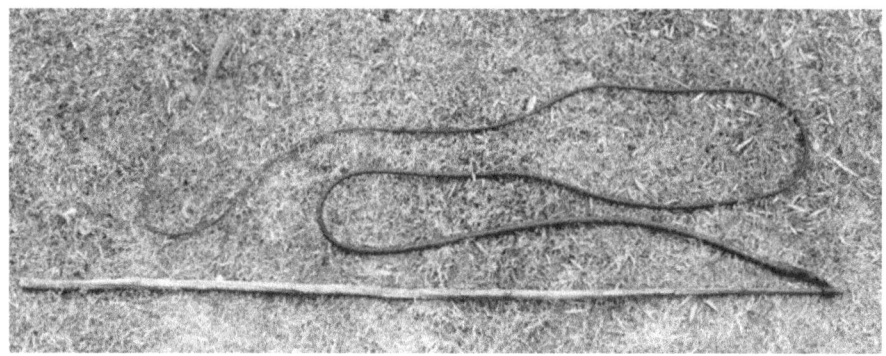

Bullock whip made by a man in Wandoan.
Handle made from lime tree.

Sam Groves' horse team and Bill English riding on logs

As the years rolled by with the wagon wheel, another wheel started in motion. Machinery slowly but surely replaced the bullock and horse teams. Trucks, being so much quicker, became popular and the art of the bullocky faded into history. The first truck to haul timber from this area was owned by Archie Baldwin.

To keep up with the trucks, chainsaws and bulldozers were used and the ability to be able to use the axe and crosscut soon disappeared.

Hoop pine was the main scrub wood that came from this area, but lying with them on the wagon and trucks were bunya pine, beech, red cedar and crow ash.

Many a story can be told of the giant forest hardwoods taken from this area.

The massive blue gums, flooded gums, yellow wood and ironbarks being hauled along the Yabba Creek Road became a common sight. When the then Irrigation and Water Supply Commission obtained land to build Borumba Dam, Buderim Lumber had the contract to remove all the sleeper timber from the area which would eventually be submerged by water. A sleeper mill was erected not far from the Bella Creek Junction School site with four men operating the mill.

As the mountains stood proud and still, they knew that this area was not for the faint-hearted or weary; and as the noise of the cutters calling "TIMBER!" and the bullocky cracking his whip changed to the buzzing of motors, they noticed it all but never said a word.

John Kropp

Crosscut saws

Blue gum log from Borumba. People in the photo from left to right: Ike Bowman, Hugh Gilroy, Hughie Bowman, Cecil Dunn, Ossie Bowman.

This blue gum log came from Schellbach's property on Little Bella Creek and was hauled to the sawmill at Buderim. People in the photo from left to right: E Barnes, R Burnett, N McGowan, R Cavanagh, L Barns, I Adams.

DAIRYING

Long before the sun rose over the hills, the hurricane lamps were lit, and the water was boiled on the wood stove for a cuppa before going to the yard to milk. The only noise heard in those early hours of the morning was the call to the cows by their owner and the dog getting abused for sending them the wrong way. The cows were milked by hand and the size of the herd depended on the size of the property. An average herd consisted of about thirty cows. As the properties were improved the herd also grew in number. The number of cows that could be milked in one hour varied, depending on the operator and the cow. Ten to twelve cows were a good average but like the fishing stories, someone was able to do just that one more.

As there was no irrigation in those days the amount of cream sent depended on the season as the landowner was at its mercy. The most popular breeds of milking cows in those years were the Jersey and Illawarra Shorthorn. The milk was separated by hand and the cream was collected in cream cans. It was then stored in a special shed called a Dairy. Every second day the cream carrier would drive his horse-drawn buckboard down the road, collecting the cream on his way. The precious cargo was unloaded at the Imbil Railway Station and then transported to the Gympie butter factory by steam train.

The summer rains and flooded creeks added to their challenge in the area. Different methods were used to take the cream across the flooded creek. Some used pack horses and carted it to the Kandanga Railway Station, while others used boats or a flying fox. The farmer always smiled during these times because he knew that his cream would be upgraded to a quality called "CHOICE" by the time it reached the factory. The reason was never known but maybe it was due to the added preservatives. As the road was improved and bridges were built across the creek, the method of milking became easier. Milking machines were invented, and it wasn't long before hand milking became a thing of the past. Trucks replaced the horse-drawn buckboard to cart the cream and the farmer had more time for growing his crops.

Cows walking out of a set of herringbone bails

As the years passed and dairying became more mechanised, this industry passed through another phase. In 1961, the factories started to change over to bulk milk and farmers had to upgrade their milking sheds to install the bulk milk vat. The cost to upgrade and the downturn in the economy forced a great number of properties to turn to other industries for their income. At present, two farmers are still dairying in this area. They are R. & P. Priebe and H. & J. Rozynski. The Illawarra Shorthorn and Jersey cattle have been phased out and replaced with the Friesian. This breed is a good milk producer and is the most popular cow for dairying at this particular time.

The dairy farmer has also reaped the benefit of a newly designed milking shed. The walk-through bails have been replaced with the herringbone bails. This new design allows more cows to be milked at one time, thus giving the farmer more time to organise his activities. The days have long passed when the cream carrier stopped to pick up his load, talk about the weather, and have a laugh. Mechanisation has taken over and milking the cow has been made much easier. But no matter what the outcome, no one will be able to replace those days when the farmer and carrier, whether in a good or poor season, worked together for that common cause of obtaining the top grade for his cream - "CHOICE".

John Kropp

Milk cans

STIRLING'S CROSSING

No story of this valley can neglect the people who came from overseas. Different people at first, they became us, enriched us, and have moved on. The 'New Australians' from war-torn Europe settled and worked at Stirling's Crossing forestry camp. These people belonged to all of us up Yabba Road.

It was after the war that refugees were given labouring jobs by the Government. Those whom the Forestry Department employed at Imbil were camped under canvas, first at the bottom of Derrier Hill, then near the creek at Stirling's Crossing – wooden floors with canvas walls and roofs. Mierochas lived for a while on the northern side of the creek. I'd ride with George Price on occasion delivering small grocery orders. I learned later that sometimes the kids got tired of Yabba fish to eat. After the big '55 flood, when most were flooded, the camp moved to higher ground near the water tower. Their new homes were palaces – made of masonite – and they were appreciated.

As I recall growing up with these children, I recall their innocence, their shy friendship, and their language disadvantage at school, which the teachers never seemed to redress. But they coped, becoming competent in English as they grew up. I recall the boys in their all-leather pants – Bavarian style. It seemed important to me as a child to learn to spell their names correctly, even though they and we had decided that they were to be pronounced as if they didn't know how to spell their own names! Talking to them today, they speak of enjoying life at Stirling's – swimming, shooting mullet, buying persimmons from Rozynskis, the lack of money and the daily trips in the school bus to civilisation. And they haven't forgotten their dislike of leather pants, their own names, being a 'migrant', and school, for all these made them 'different' and they were sensitive to this subtle alienation.

But they went to the bush Sunday School, they found aboriginal tools near the bora ground, and went for rides with the Catholic priest when he came to conduct Mass. They recall the big '55 flood when they had to evacuate to the 'big house' (the four permanent ones) and then clean out mud afterwards. But they became even closer as a community after that.

Ian Stehbens

YABBA CREEK SLEEPER MILL

In late 1961, a sleeper mill was set up at the intersection of Yabba Creek and Bella Creek Roads. Mr. Arn Barnes, Manager and part owner of Buderim Lumber, had put in a tender for all suitable sleeper timber from the Borumba Dam site.

The sawmill consisted of an overhead Canadian, a bench, a docking saw and saw sharpening equipment. A four-man crew operated the sawmill. Most of the logs were broken down on a rack, with two sleepers being taken from each log.

The railway quota was for 40,000 sleepers but the timber on the dam site was exhausted after 10,000 sleepers were cut. Buderim Lumber then had to buy timber privately. The bulk of this timber came from the Sinnamon and Schellbach properties. The main sleeper timber was ironbark and some grey gum. There were also some large blue gum logs taken from the Schellbach property to be used in the Buderim Sawmill.

The method used for getting these logs out was to winch the bulldozer up onto the ledges, push the logs over the side, and pick up what we could find at the bottom. It was quite successful as we only lost track of about three logs and Mr. Schellbach didn't have much lantana left on his hill when we were finished. We also had a Blitz truck to cart the logs and sleepers. Two men were swinging on the water bag carrier to get up the hill at Sinnamons. We would put half a load of sleeper logs on the truck and snig two logs down the range to be cut into lengths and loaded at the bottom. We always had a man on hand with a bottle of water to put out the handbrake fire halfway down the hill, as the oil around it would catch fire.

The original sleeper mill crew were Merv Harland (benchman), Brian Cavanagh (tailerout), Ted Barnes (docker), Ralph Dean (saw doctor and part owner) later replaced by Herb Jones (benchman), Russell Cavanagh (tailerout), and Bill Barnes (saw doctor and business partner).

However, the time at Yabba Creek was not without tragedy as one of the timber cutters, Wally Croker, was killed when he felled a tree on himself at the Borumba Dam site. Mr. Andy Adams of Imbil was responsible for carting the sleepers and firewood away from the sleeper mill.

Ted Barnes

GLENVEAGH – VIA IMBIL

Glenveagh cattle property, fourteen miles from Imbil, was bought by Myles MacDonnell in 1952 from Mr. Louis Horne. The only building on the property was a one- roomed hut with an outside galley. In those years it was virtually a track from the Bella Creek turn-off, with nine creek crossings.

During a period of wet seasons, it was not uncommon to have a vehicle stranded for two to three months at a time, so supplies had to be brought in by packhorse from Kandanga Creek side. We joined Oakwood on the eastern side – on the west, Yabba Station (then managed by "Boy" McDonald) and Kingaham, owned by the Moore family, then later Peter Webster.

The inaccessibility of roads meant cattle for market were driven to Kandanga truckyards, or Gympie sale yards, via Kandanga, Amamoor and Glastonbury.

There was no power or phone, but later a party line was erected by us and the Atthow family.

Change came in the early 1960s when Borumba Dam started. The timber was hauled out, therefore the roads had to be improved.

Borumba was like a little township. Its main attraction was the 'canteen', which was run by 'personality' Johnny Myrob, who later was publican of the Queens Hotel, Gympie.

Various men worked on Glenveagh with us: Mick Murphy, well-known in campdrafting and racing circles, Peter Clauson, now manager of a large property in the Northern Territory, Charlie Portas, Mick Morley, Ray Shanahan, Monty Smalley, Snow Herrington and Percy Conlan, who was accidentally killed on the property.

We have good memories of visits from Harold Rush, G. Veitch, Fred Pidgeon, Sergeant McGrath, the Atthow family, Bill Low, Clarrie Nichols, Shirley and Joe McFarlane.

The biggest social function on Glenveagh was when Rucide was installed in the dip by the well-known ICI traveller of that era, Arthur Anderson.

Sheelagh MacDonnell

GLENVEAGH – BELLA CREEK ROAD, VIA IMBIL

R.M. and L.J. Benham acquired 'Glenveagh' in September 1978. R.M. Benham was raised at Gayndah and L.J. in the pearling town of Broome, Western Australia.

'Glenveagh' is run by Bill and Jennifer Benham. Bill is originally from Geebung in Brisbane but spent six years at Longreach Pastoral College and surrounding properties in the Blackall area. Jennifer, a trained nurse, is from the seaside town of Lennox Head in northern New South Wales.

The 10,000-acre property was running pure Hereford cattle at the time of purchase but now has a Brahman cross. A few of the Hereford breeders still remain on the property. Brahmans have improved the herd and saved many hours of mustering and dipping, leaving more time for improvements in other areas.

Deer farming was commenced as a sideline in 1979. It has untapped potential that may help to create a new industry for Queensland and being in a feral area of quite large herds of wild deer, it was decided to farm them.

Being a new venture, it has been a headache at times, but much has been learned by trial and error about these unique and interesting animals - their likes, dislikes and habits.

Although the Benhams have been there for ten years they have yet to experience the 'BIG WET' they've heard of. Only on a few occasions have they been caught here by rising creeks.

The telephone line was a single, rusty wire strung from tree to tree and with every wind and storm, it would break. Many hours were spent fixing it. It was almost impossible to hear or be heard. Upgrading to the telephone with an underground cable took place in 1982. Hooray!

Bill and Jennifer Benham now have two children, both born in Nambour. Katie, five years old, attends Imbil State School, and David who is three years old.

MANTHEY'S PROPERTY

Rudolph Charles (Charlie) Manthey was born in Prussia in 1863. He sailed on the ship, 'La Rochelle', and arrived at Moreton Bay on the 25th December 1865. He married Augusta Henrietta Willersdorf on the 1st August 1891. They had ten children.

His wife died in October 1904, at age thirty-six. His eldest daughter, Annie Mary, reared the younger children. She then married Albert Ernst at Bollier.

Charlie Manthey bought the property at Bella Creek about 1913. It was on a square mile or 640 acres. He grazed cattle and cut timber. He built a two-storey building to camp in during the week but actually lived in Imbil the rest of the time.

It appears he shifted to Imbil in 1917. The same year, one son died in a shooting accident at Imbil. Another son was killed by rolling logs at the Imbil railway yard in 1923.

They would take a bullock team up one day and bring a load of logs back to Imbil the next day. They would do this about twice a week. Logs were hoop and bunya pine. The property was sold to William Lowe in the 1930s.

Bunya log from this Bella Creek property
hauled to the Imbil Railway Station

PORTION 70 – PARISH IMBIL

This article was written after an interview with Mr. Ted Schellbach who lived on a property on Little Bella Creek and is now retired at Power Road, Southside, Gympie. The dialogue is not word for word as per the interview but the information in this article is a true account of those bygone days on that property.

Anybody home?" "Yes."

"Ted Schellbach?" "Yes, that's me.

"My name is John Kropp. You wouldn't know me, but I am a member of a group of people who are getting together to organise a reunion for people who lived and worked on properties along Yabba Creek and its tributaries from Kropps Crossing. I was told that you lived in the area, and I was wondering if you could tell me a little about this property."

"Oh yes, well what would you like to know then?"

"I suppose the best place to start is at the beginning. How did you come by the land?"

"Well, I obtained the land by ballot. Do you know what I mean when I say by ballot?"

"That's when the government advertises a block of land and people put their names in a box and if your name is drawn out then the land becomes yours."

"More or less. It's a bit more involved than that, but that's close enough. We moved to that block on Little Bella Creek in about 1921. There was so much timber on the place we had to clean an area to build a house—wasn't a house like I'm living in now either. Bill Simpson, my son- in-law, cut some timber on my place to build his house at Imbil. I remember one log had 3000 super feet in the butt. It took him a couple of days to cut it down too. He rode up on his horse one Sunday morning and worked on the tree all day and then came back the following weekend and finished it off. No chainsaws in those days, young fellow, just the crosscut saw and axe."

"I was told that you had dairy cattle on the place." "We sure did."

"How many cows did you milk?"

"The wife and I started off by milking twelve cows, but as the land was cleared, we increased our herd to 120 cows. We milked by hand until milking machines came on the market, and it wasn't long before we had a unit installed. Mind you, as the farm was being developed our family increased and this made things easier."

"How many children in the family?"

"There were three girls and four boys. Bill was the eldest, then Wilfred, Joyce, Evelyn, Mavis, Roy and Eric."

"Rumour has it that you were the cream carrier for this end of the creek, and you started off by carting the cream in a buckboard drawn by horses."

"That's right. Every Monday, Wednesday and Friday, the horses were hitched up to the buckboard and the cream was carted to the Imbil Railway Station. Through the summer months, an extra trip was taken on Saturdays. The old buckboard was full by the time I loaded the last can of cream. After unloading the cream, I would pick up the farmers' grocery order at the store and deliver them on the way home. I wouldn't like to try and count the number of cups of tea I had while delivering the groceries. By joves, those cuppas and scones were good! Could those women cook!"

"What did you do with the cream while the creek was in flood?"

"We stored it in the dairy shed. Sometimes we would take it across on packhorses to Kandanga. Boats were also used. Everyone along the creek took part in transporting the cream from one crossing to the other. That Deep Crossing was the worst one to cross. I didn't like going through that one when the creek started to rise. In a normal time, the water was well up the horse's legs."

"What did you live on when you couldn't get supplies?"

"My boy, a lot of the food came in bulk in those days. You could buy flour in 150lb bags and sugar came in 70lb bags. We baked our own bread, ate corn beef until you nearly went the colour of it, and we always grew a few vegetables. Mind you, if the meat supply was getting low, we used to shoot a pigeon or two and make pigeon soup. Good tucker too, I might add."

"Was dairying the only industry carried out on this property?"

"No. We had our own case mill up there for a while. The lads and I worked it, and we sold the cases to the local pineapple growers."

"What type of timber did you make the cases out of?"

"Flooded gum—made good cases too. I don't think they use cases anymore in the pineapples."

"No, they don't. All the pineapples sent to the cannery go in big bins and the fresh pineapples for the markets are packed into cardboard cartons. Have you any photos of those days that I could have a look at?"

"No. Hardly anyone had a camera then, not like today, everyone seems to have one. I do have a photo of a bunya log on a wagon here, somewhere. The log came off Manthey's property, which was beside mine, and the photo was given to me. Most of the pictures taken in my time were taken with a Box Brownie. They were a strange looking camera, but they did the job. Just hang on and I'll see if I can find that photo."

A long time elapsed before Ted spoke again but when he did, the following words came loud and clear.

"I wonder where I put that bloody photo?" "Don't worry. It doesn't really matter."

Ted came back to his chair mumbling under his breath and disappointed.

"Who did you sell your property to?"

"A chap by the name of Sinnamon bought in 1960 and I moved to Woolooga to live for a while and then bought a property at The Dawn and then retired here at Southside."

"Well, it's been interesting talking with you Mr. Schellbach. Will you be coming to the reunion day on the 7th May?"

"Depends on my health. You know I'll be ninety-five on the 5th of May this year, but I'll see what I can do."

John Kropp

ATTHOW FAMILY

In the beginning, the land we now occupy was taken up by the Swansons at Yabba and the Elworthys and Mellors of Imbil Station. 'Bella Springs,' where we reside, was freeholded by Elworthys and Mellors as were the freehold blocks on Callemondah, which my father, Bert Atthow, purchased in 1927 from August Loweke, and one area of perpetual lease where the home and improvements now stand.

In 1927 we moved over from Kilcoy. My grandfather bought country in this district around 1908 or earlier which comprised Kingaham, Oakwood, Borgan, and Glen Idol. Various blocks were put into various names of his family. Glen Idol was purchased from MacGills in 1918 with huts, plus dip and yards. Patterson's block, approximately 5000 acres, was also in the deal. MacGills had previously swapped the Borumba property, which was originally taken up and developed by Newton McLean, for Patterson's block.

Wire paddock was purchased from Beausangs and top and bottom Stantons from the Stantons. This area, except the original Glen Idol block of 2946 acres, is now owned by the Benham family and is called Glenveagh. Glen Idol was originally selected by Doc Edwards who used to breed horses and sell them in New South Wales. He was reputed to have bred the famous Outlaw of Glen Idol which a lady, who used to help him train his horses, would ride.

As time went on, I purchased 1200 acres from Yabba Station, 2000 odd acres from Taylors, originally Bill and Ivy Lowes, and 700 acres from Joyce Rush, country originally selected by F.E. Schellbach (Schelly), our first cream carter and mail contractor. This country was the last put up for selection under the Moore government in the early '30s. This is now our 'Bella Springs' – 'Glen Idol' cattle property.

Ray Atthow

ATTHOW FAMILY

On July 12, 1927, at 8.30 p.m. we arrived at the back door of our new home, 'Callemondah'. 'Callemondah' means surrounded by hills and was chosen by my late mother, Helen Atthow. The blocks comprising Callemondah were Portion 68, where the house now stands, and Portions 1190 and 1250 - a total of 640 acres.

The previous owner was Augustus Wilhelm Loweke, a widower with three daughters, who, after their mother's death, boarded in Gympie. The previous house, a cottage, was originally on Portion 1190 but when Portion 68 was selected, it was moved there. It was a condition of selection that the owner must reside on his block for five years and fruit trees had to be planted.

We arrived in a buggy pulled by two brown/bay horses, Monitor and Marcus. We had come from our Kilcoy home up Yednia Range, through Yabba and Kingaham stations, and down the present route from Mt Buggery. Our spring cart drawn by the old grey, Bulcher, was also brought with the aviary of mother's canaries and round tubs from the wash house filled with fifty rose bushes. The roses came from the beautiful garden of Highwood, Kilcoy, which had been selected by my grandfather, G.A. Atthow in 1902.

The first dip in the Kilcoy area was built about this time marking the arrival of the cattle tick in Queensland. Around this time a dip was built at the Borgan which had been selected in 1886 by Thomas Walker. Walker's Top, the highest point, still bears his name.

The Borgan was held by a person named Carter from approximately 1902 to 1912 when the actual transfer was made to my grandfather. This land has been held continually by my family since that time and

I am the third generation to hold it.

Portions 469 and 1189 were later acquired by my father from Albert William Lowe, who also owned Bollier Station, now Tuncul Park. These portions were purchased in August 1933 with Portion 1189 being the block where my brother now resides with his family.

The buggy and horses we arrived with were lent to F.E. Schellbach by my dad and played a large part in the original cream run from Little Bella Creek. A small chestnut horse was used for the initial mail run with people expecting mail to be delivered in impossible conditions. In those days of no main roads or bridges, the law stated that the agent was not compelled to ride over a stream deeper than the tip of his saddle flaps beneath the stirrups. From 1914 to about 1960, the only postmaster in Imbil was H. Smith.

Three landholders, C. Neucom, L.J Horne and Bert Atthow, undertook to build a party line from Imbil to our property. With eleven subscribers on a single line, it could be quite fun, especially if Dad ran in to order a permit or to deliver cattle and had to wait for two gossiping women to finish. Sometimes, if the matter was urgent, you had to excuse yourself and ask if you could make a call.

Invariably after floods or storms, the lines would be damaged and had to be maintained by private labour. The public box which hung forbiddingly on a tall pole opposite Louis Horne's gate was to be touched only by the PMG and they were never in a hurry.

Our first school was built as a Provisional School where an attendance of fourteen had to be maintained to keep it open. Four teachers were engaged in the few years it operated. We boarded the teachers together with Mrs. Becker and Mrs. Donald at different intervals. The school was built with donations of timber by my dad and others and carpenter F.E Schellbach. Five children were enrolled on the first day.

When the school closed down through a lack of pupils, it was purchased by Bert Atthow and moved to its present site. Two pine trees are still standing on the old site from five planted one Arbour Day.

Shirley McFarlane

Plunge dip at the Borgan showing the shingle roof later covered with an iron roof

Cattle grazing on the Borgan country

THE ANGUS HERD (THREE GENERATIONS)

Sixty-five years ago, at 'Highwood,' Kilcoy - country selected by the Atthow family in 1902 - was the beginning of a new herd of cattle for the Atthow empire. Later it was worth a total of a quarter million pounds approximately before the crash after the 1914-18 war. This empire later fell apart when the founder, George Albert Atthow, gave up the reins to the younger generation. The four sons then went their own ways.

In 1923 my grandfather purchased the first Aberdeen Angus stud bull at the Brisbane exhibition as he wanted to depart from the straight Hereford cattle originally run on all properties. The Herefords had been quite successful but had developed a tendency to cancer eyes which the harsh Queensland climate did not help. For the next four years, these cattle were bred at Kilcoy.

In 1927, my father, the third son, decided to go it alone on Angus because he liked them so much. Having country at the Borgan, he moved to Imbil on our present site and continued to concentrate on full Angus. He bought mainly herd bulls to start (as they were less expensive) to obtain a foundation herd of breeders, crossing mostly with shorthorn cattle which produced better and fatter calves, thus making for better conformation in breeding cattle.

As the Angus colour is so strong and overrules most other colours, he was able to breed good, heavy- producing, big-bodied cows.

From this beginning he could later afford to buy some stud females and better stud bulls to infuse the whole herd, producing a type of Angus beast which over the years has been particularly successful in our rough country, so similar to the breed's country of origin in Scotland.

When my father passed on in 1962, the herd was shared by my brother and myself. His share was carried on for about four or five years and then he introduced Santa Gertrudis. I was very keen to continue with Angus which I have until today, making the present herd sixty-five years deep.

I consider them the supreme breed for temperament and rapid weight gain in comparison to other breeds. Nothing is more appealing than the sight of a mob of straight blacks against the green surrounding our valleys and hills. In earlier times, until about 1945, all of our fat stock were sent to saleyards at Cannon Hill in Brisbane. They were driven by road and horseback firstly to Traveston for some time and later to Pomona railway station where they were loaded and railed to Brisbane. The journey took two days from home to sale yard.

After leaving our property, Callemondah, at about 11.30

a.m. on a Tuesday, Bert would walk his stock to Bollier, a distance of twelve miles the first day. At 3 a.m. the next morning, the journey continued to the Pomona station where they were loaded about 11 a.m. for the seven-hour journey. The men then returned to our property about 5 p.m.

During the late 1930s, the first livestock carrier, P.J. Andreassen from Bollier, started with motor trucks. He carried pigs and calves to Gympie sale yards for auction. Later, he acquired larger trucks to carry fat stock to the Gympie auctions on Thursdays. The beginning of this new era in our district proved a blessing to all but ended the practice of cattle droving in the march of progress.

In the years before the war (WWII), my brother and I had to drove bullocks to the local butcher every Saturday morning. We left home at 6 a.m. and delivered the stock to the slaughter yard paddock at

Brooloo, then owned by the Gomersall brothers.

Fat bullocks, of three or four years of age, at one stage fetched only six or seven pounds a head at a good sale. Thank goodness the values improved.

The Gomersall brothers were in Imbil as butchers for many years before the Second World War. They pioneered electric light in Imbil township by supplying power from their generators.

Ray, Tabby and Clive Gomersall, with puppies

PORTION 7 PARISH IMBIL – DEEP CREEK CROSSING, YABBA CREEK

This farm, comprising 212 acres was first settled by George and Bertha Saunders in 1918. The property has seen many changes since those early days.

During its history, owners have tried various types of farming. Small crops were grown on the southern slopes and on the flats. Grapes were grown for a short time, also on the flats.

Dairying played a major part on the property for a time, as Yabba Creek was well known for its dairy farms.

In 1978, pheasants and guinea fowl were raised as table birds for sale to restaurants, both local and interstate.

Land was cleared for growing bananas in a sheltered valley of this property in the early days.

At present, on the western slope of this valley, we are quarrying slate. After twelve months of preliminary work to establish the quarry, we are now in a position to sell slate to landscapers. The slate comes from the Amamoor bed and is some of the hardest slate in the Gympie area. We are quarrying the slate from vertical beds. When sediment originally collects, it is layered horizontally. Over time, earth movement forces some to the vertical.

The slate is found on approximately one-third of the property, but it is hard to get at. It has taken many hours of hard work with heavy machinery to gain access to the quarry.

The labour-intensive process starts with light blasting followed by work with a jackhammer. The slate is split using a hammer and bolster and air tools. It has many colours and is ideal for outdoor landscaping.

Mary Valley Slate Quarry is owned and operated by Ted and Maureen Barnes and their children Joanne, Kylie and Scott.

Previous owners of this property have been Daniel McBride, Arnold Borg, John Olliof, Ivan Dakin, Jonn and James Humphries, Frank and Jean Brown.

Ted and Maureen Barnes

BILLY FRIENDS' FARM PORTION 12 PARISH IMBIL – COUNTY LENNOX

Billy Friends' farm was five and a half miles from Imbil on the Yabba Creek at the fifth crossing. It was a selection of 126 acres with a one-mile creek frontage in the shape of a horseshoe. Another selection and the forestry were on its boundaries.

It was a returned soldier's selection after World War One. The government of the day opened up crown land for soldiers to settle. They made small yearly payments over long terms, then they could pay the balance to make it freehold property.

The country was scrub and forest with the soil ranging from sandy loam to red volcanic soil. Bullock teams made the start of the roads – the original road being just below the house. Motor transport brought the bridges out as far as Friends' Crossing. The first bridge was a spider bridge – two runners across the creek wide enough apart for the trucks to cross. There were no planks in the centre. They were very useful in flood times to take out the cream can and bring in supplies.

As the selection was cleared, some of the trees were used to make a small home and outbuildings.

Remember, it was horse and cart days, so the house was small with verandas back and front, one bedroom and a living room in the centre. The back veranda was boarded up and made into half kitchen and half eating, work room or you name it! There were front and back steps and one water tank. The laundry was outside with a copper boiler and two big tubs to wash or bath in. Laundry was done by hand with a rubbing board, a bar of homemade soap and plenty of hard labour.

Trees of no use were ringbarked and left to die. Scrub was chopped down and burnt and grass was planted. A dairy was started. Cultivation was mainly for farm use. Small crops grown were corn, potatoes, pumpkin, oats, lucerne, turnips, arrowroot and cow cane. After World War Two, pineapples were tried but more was made out of beans and peas that were grown between the rows. Pigs were always a good sideline.

Lighting for the home and power-driven engines were run on petrol or kerosene. The most often used and safest light was the kerosene hurricane which could be hung up, carried, or just sat.

Cream was first carted into Imbil by horse and on to the Gympie factory three times a week. Later it was taken by two separate carters to Gympie or Pomona – the two factories were rivals.

Billy Friend was the selector. He leased to Raymonds. Friend returned and worked the farm until he sold to Nicholsons.

George Nicholson

PORTION 12, PARISH IMBIL – COUNTY LENNOX

In July 1977, we purchased the property from Mr. and Mrs. Sunderhoff. It had been a dairy and piggery. We moved here from Caloundra with our four children, Tony, Kerry, Vicky and Donna, with the intention of starting a deer farm.

As this was a very new venture for Queensland, it has taken a few years to set up and develop the property as a commercial deer farm. The biggest expense was, of course, fencing. To farm deer, you must have all your external fences six feet six inches high. Good drinking water and wallow holes in each paddock are other essentials as well as strong suitable yards for working deer. The yards must be undercover as deer handle better in a dull light. 3

There is a steady market for live sales of all breeds of deer. The antler from the stag is harvested in the velvet stage and sold, mainly on the Asian market. It is used in medicines. Queensland has also developed excellent venison (deer meat) outlets and we sell stags to supply this market.

Our initial stock was Red deer, trapped in the local area, which proved good foundation stock. In the past few years, we have branched out into tropical deer which are more suited to our conditions. We have purchased Javan Rusa, Moluccan Rusa and Chital breeds.

We are now concentrating on upgrading our stock with good-quality breeding hinds and stags.

In 1981 we subdivided the property which was divided by Yabba Creek Road and these two parts are now Portion 1 and 2.

TIMES TO REMEMBER

We sold Portion 1 (adjoining the Church of England Girls Grammar School) to John Stabb the same year. John has since sold the property to his brother David.

In 1983, we planted a custard apple orchard, and these are now bearing marketable fruit.

The original pigsties are now used for storage and deer shelters and the big shed has been partly converted to deer yards.

Where the original settlers on this property spent many hours clearing the land to plant crops for grazing, we have spent hours planting many hundreds of trees for shelter for the deer.

Where the original farmers tried to discourage the wild deer from eating their crops, we planted crops, in traps, to encourage the wild deer. History always seems to go the full circle.

Rick and June Gibson

SUB 2 PORTION 870 – PARISH BROOLOO

Boardman Farm, which had been part of Imbil Station, was bought by Harry Boardman around the beginning of the First World War. The 120-acre farm consisted of black forest flats with scrub in the gullies. Corn was grown with some other crops. Harry lived in a one- roomed dwelling where the cow yards are today. He then built a small, two-story home with the help of Jack Shore. He married Winifred Bradshaw who worked for Ernest Nicholls on what was to become Garrett's farm.

In the early twenties, a dairy was started. In addition, pigs were kept and crops raised.

After the Second World War, Harry's son, Bill, took over for a few years and then sold to Cook and Thomson who later sold to Ray Smith.

As a young man, Harry Boardman did fencing for Alex Andrews (now Priebe's). He split the posts and put them in the ground one-third of their length. Some are still standing after seventy years.

Fishing with handlines in Yabba Creek was popular. Large cod up to forty pounds were caught as well as jew (catfish), eels and turtles. Jew and cod were good eating especially when floods were on, and supplies were getting short. Worms were used for bait, dug from the creek bank. Barramundi and lungfish were caught. Lungfish, with pale pink flesh, was first boiled in milk and then fried in the usual way. Mullet too was plentiful and in the early days was blown with dynamite.

Great picnics were held on the creek. Families came in sulkies, subbies and on horseback. The billy boiled for tea on an open fire and lovely food was plentiful. We had swimming and games. Mums and dads joined in too. Oh, what fun! Watermelon skin fights were enjoyed by the children too.

One of the ways we earned a few pence was by having a rat and mouse hunt. Because of all the corn in the barn, rats and mice were plentiful. It was great fun hunting with the help of our blue dog. We were given one penny for a rat and one penny for three mice. Good money considering a loaf of bread was then four pence.

Mr. & Mrs. Harry Boardman on their new tractor

SMALL RECOLLECTIONS

Mr. Stirling made yokes by hand for the bullock teams. He had a building at Stirling's Crossing.

Henry Boardman had a property at the top end of Bella Creek that he used for a dry run. It was very steep. He grew fruit up there after the Second World War.

May Nicholson (nee Boardman)

SUB 2 PORTION 870 – PARISH BROOLOO

Ray and Enid Smith and sons Bevan (four) and Lloyd (one) purchased the Yabba Creek property 'Broadacres' from the Cook and Thomson families in the drought year of 1951. They brought with them Ayrshire cattle and draught horses. The horses were worked on cultivation in conjunction with a tractor until well into the sixties.

The first of two daughters, Janelle, was born in 1953 and Kerry arrived in 1966. Bevan, Lloyd and Janelle all attended Imbil State School being transported by the Yabba Creek bus.

In the early fifties the farm income was from the sale of cream and pigs and feed grown was probably oats for the dairy cows and corn, pumpkins and turnips for the pigs.

The mid-fifties saw many big floods and the long monsoon seasons resulted in properties being flood- bound for days. As floodwaters receded, the locals used flying foxes to ferry their cream cans across creeks. One flying fox was on Yabba Creek, crossing number five, but probably every crossing had one.

Ray showed cattle from his 'Rocklea' Ayrshire stud at Imbil and Gympie. In 1955 he introduced the Guernsey breed and founded the 'Remleigh' stud. 'Remleigh' was derived from Enid's maiden name, Remington.

About fifty acres of cultivation was sown to annual crops in the fifties – mainly oats, cowpeas, corn, pumpkins, turnips and the odd crop of peanuts.

The early sixties saw the introduction of a small diesel-powered irrigation plant which allowed the planting of dairy pastures such as lucerne, clover and prairie grass. Hay baling machinery was purchased, and the first fodder was conserved during this period. The DPI conducted a field day on the property in about 1963 centred around milk production from irrigated improved pastures.

The early sixties were the change over from cream and separated milk to whole milk production for Kraft cheeses at Kenilworth. Pigs were then reared on whey and grain and calves on milk replacers.

The mid-sixties saw the Remleigh herd excel in milk and butter-fat production and exhibit at the Brisbane Royal Show. Until Ray's untimely death in 1968, a total of two champions and three reserve champions had been shown. Since then, the Remleigh prefix has figured in a host of Royal Champions.

"Remleigh" Brightlight
Champ Guernsey and Supreme Champ Dairy Cow
Bred and Shown by Est. R.J. Smith, Imbil
(First Guernsey to be Supreme at an Australian Royal Show)

A tribute to Ray's breeding program was realised in 1970 when Enid and family gained the Supreme Dairy Cow award at Brisbane with 'Brightlight', thus being the first Guernsey cow in Australia to be judged 'Supreme' at a Royal Show.

The property after 1968 was owned by Enid until about 1970 when it was purchased by Lloyd and his wife, Bobby. They, with their two children, Brett and Joanne, carried on dairying and introduced small crops such as beans, zucchinis, gherkins, cucumbers and sweet corn.

In the mid-eighties, half of the property consisting of the house block and the dairy herd was sold. Lloyd retains the flats and continues to grow small crops.

Enid and Kerry and Janelle (Hewitt) now live in Gympie and Bevan lives and works in Samford.

Bevan Smith

Header, harvesting beans

ANDREASSEN – PORTION 168043
LOT 1 – PARISH BROOLOO

In 1960, 121 acres covering both sides of Yabba Road were bought by Peter Andreassen from Buller Doyle and used mainly for dairying and corn growing.

A house was moved from the Imbil Forestry to its present location in 1968 and renovated during 1976-77.

Peter and his son Trevor began growing ginger with three acres in 1969 and steadily increased this quota to twenty-three acres in 1983. A world depression made the industry unviable and ginger production ceased in that year.

Processing beans were grown for Wattie-Pict and Edgell's from 1976 to 1980 with mixed success. Other small crops were also grown during this time.

The cultivations on the farm went under water in the July 1973 flood and again in January 1974 when two acres of ginger and irrigation pipes were washed away.

When Peter passed away in 1975, the farm was handed down to Trevor who moved to the farm in 1977 with his wife Dorothy and their two sons Barry and Michael. A third son, David, was born in 1979.

The property was subdivided into 3 lots in 1979 with lots 2 and 3 across the road from the house being sold to Vince and Anna Vagner and Ian Rackham.

Since ginger production ceased, the property has been used for grazing and as a workshop and base for Trevor's backhoe and earth-moving business.

ANDREASSEN – BUTLERS CORNER

Peter and Mary Andreassen took over the Forestry Lease on Butlers Corner in 1951 and had share-farmers on the dairy until they moved there themselves in July 1959.

Peter and Mary and their sons ran the dairy until 1974 (Mary passed away in 1971) when the forestry reclaimed the lease for tree planting. The house was moved to Ballard Road, Imbil and the machinery and other equipment moved to the property at No. 4 crossing on Yabba Road. Peter operated a livestock-carrying business from Butlers Corner during this time also.

During the construction of Borumba Dam traffic was often diverted through Butlers Corner to avoid the low creek crossings at Nos. 2 and 3 on Yabba Road during periods of wet weather.

SUB 4 PORTION 870 – PARISH BROOLOO

Our property which is situated on the banks of Yabba Creek with little Derrier Creek running through it, was originally part of the Imbil Station. The station which comprised 14000 acres included Bollier Flats, Bergin's Pocket, Imbil Township and acres of rich Yabba Creek flats extending to Bella and Derrier Creeks. It used to run 6000 or more head of Hereford cattle.

The Imbil Estate was listed for sale by public auction at the Homestead on March 17th 1914. It was subdivided into fifty-seven farms ranging in size from eighty to 799 acres. Also, 100 township allotments were offered.

Our farm, Sub 4 of Portions 870 and 1153 Parish of Brooloo, was originally selected by Mr. Andrew Becker who together with his wife and children, Jack and Molly, engaged in the timber and dairying industries. Though the bullocks had long gone, evidence of the farmer was still apparent when we moved to the area in 1946. A piece off a bullock wagon, a stray bullock bow or key would be unearthed or located in some unexpected place throughout the farm, still clearly recognisable.

After several years Mr. Becker sold to Mr. Bill Parkinson who with his family carried on the dairying business. He sold to Mr. Robert Chapple (Bob). Mr. Chapple, his wife May and son Douglas remained on the property for five years when ill health forced him to sell. Douglas joined the police force but unfortunately, Mr. Chapple's health was such that he did not enjoy many years of retirement.

Harry and I bought the farm off the Chapples and took over on June

19th 1946. Harry had recently been discharged from the armed forces in which he served for three and a half years during World War II.

As the war had only been over for a short time, fencing material and machinery of any description were practically unprocurable. Consequently, it was a case of mend and make do, or substitute.

Any cultivation that was done had to be done by horses, a very slow process when compared with today's modern equipment.

Mr. Gordon Milfull was our cream carrier. The cream was picked up at the farm in fine weather, but in wet weather, the horse had to be yoked up and the cream taken out to the road by slide. Mr. Milfull also delivered the mail three times a week and any goods necessary.

There were quite a number of dairy farmers along the creek. Today there are two, Robin Priebe and ourselves.

Wallabies were our share farmers. We would plant a crop and they would practically harvest it for us, leaving our animals very little.

In 1951, we purchased sufficient wire netting to enclose the whole farm, thus eliminating the wallaby problem and also the dingo to a large extent.

With the enclosure, we decided to purchase some sheep. We had over 400 at times, which over the years included Merino, Romney, Marsh, Border Leicester, Southdown and Suffolk. The Merinos were a poor investment as they did not thrive in this country. The hardier breeds did very well, and we had no trouble in disposing of the lambs to the local markets. In fact, the butchers would tell us they kept our lamb only for their very favoured customers, especially the Southdowns who are a very popular breed for the fat lamb market. The sheep were sold to Nambour, Tewantin and Gympie with the buyers often sending a truck to pick them up.

The sheep paddocks were subdivided with ringlock wire. Drenching and crutching were done at the appropriate times with Harry doing the shearing in the spring. The fleeces, while not first class, yielded some very satisfactory prices. We kept the sheep for about eighteen years. When wool prices dropped, we decided to concentrate exclusively on dairying.

Pineapples were grown on a few acres of our property by one of the new Australians who worked in the forestry. He did the work on weekends and his wife worked lots of days during the week, with children assisting when possible.

This particular family never failed to show their gratitude. The pineapple was a great help in establishing them here in their adopted country.

Our property is bounded on two sides by the Imbil State Forestry. When we first came to the district, there was a small camp of forestry workers, with their families, camped at our back fence. There were also other small camps scattered throughout the forestry.

A couple of years later a new forestry officer arrived in Imbil to take charge of the area. He decided instead of having their employees so scattered, to make one big community so the forestry could look after their workers and their families and give them a much better service. This idea culminated in the camp being made at Stirling's Crossing not very far from our front gate. It grew to be quite a sizeable camp with the single men's barracks on one side of the road and the married men's quarters on the opposite side.

It was at this site that our three children, Walter, Norma and Gary, with a number of children from the camp boarded the school bus each morning to attend the Imbil State School. There were a number of new Australians in this camp. They came from various parts of Europe and the British Isles under the post-war immigration scheme.

Gay times were enjoyed in the recreation hall in the form of Christmas parties, dances and other forms of entertainment. This camp has now closed, and the area has practically returned to its natural state, making it hard to believe it was once home to so many folks. As electricity did not come to the area until approximately 1954, milking was carried out with the aid of a kerosene engine. This engine could be very temperamental. Hot water was obtained from an outdoor fire. A chip heater was later installed. Household lighting was in the form of kerosene lights and ironing was done with 'Mrs Potts' or a petrol iron. With the advent of electricity and Borumba Dam opening in 1964, we were ensured of a continuous water supply, thereby making it practicable to install underground mains at strategic points throughout the farm for the purpose of irrigation and improved pastures. No doubt this farm has seen major changes since the days when Aborigines roamed the area.

In this the Bicentennial year, we are constantly reminded of the progress that has taken place since white man came to our shores. We can but ponder as to what changes will occur on our farm during the next two centuries.

Jess Rozynski

PORTION 438 – PARISH OF IMBIL

The Krause family worked Andrew's farm (now owned by Priebes) from 1928 to 1931. Jack was the eldest, Les was sixteen and had finished high school in Toowoomba. Eric and Paddy rode ponies to Imbil School and Beryl was a toddler. Only recently, Paddy admitted to doing a lot of wagging from school after Eric finished but was never found out at the time. Eighty cows were milked by hand, about one hundred pigs were kept for fattening, and sixty acres of corn were grown each year. All the family helped with milking. Jack kept a large vegetable garden and Les was the ploughman. He could plough three acres a day, using a two-furrow disc plough pulled by three horses. All the land was ploughed twice and harrowed after each ploughing. The corn was pulled by hand, and what was not sold was stored in tanks for pig and horse feed.

Mr. Krause (Cap) and Jack picked together, filling seven cartloads a day, giving about fifty bags of shelled corn. They would milk in the morning but would keep on pulling during the evening milking. Three men worked with the wagon – Scotchy English, Walter Groves and Squeaker Robson. The crop averaged sixty bushels to the acre, and prices were about 3/6 to 4/- (35c to 40c) per bushel. Albert Barsby carted it to Imbil Railway yards for 6d (5c) per three-bushel bag. It was not hybrid corn, and seed was saved each year for next year's crop planting. No fertiliser was used.

About two acres of arrowroot were grown for pig feed each year and three to five acres of both pumpkins and English potatoes for sale. Each day arrowroot would be dug and boiled in a big cast-iron boiler ready for feeding pigs the next day. While corn pulling was in progress, ploughing for next year's crops was also done.

The cream was taken to Imbil to go by rail to Gympie. In flood time it was boated across the creek at Stirling's Crossing. One year it had to be boated constantly for six weeks as the creek was uncrossable for vehicles. Strangely, no lucerne was grown and chaff was bought for horse feed. Pigs had to be taken to Brooloo to be loaded, first in a T-model Ford truck, later in a Rugby truck.

RECREATION

TENNIS – A court was built at Butler's Corner and the White Rose Club played there. The court builders were Jack Donald, Alf Tincknell, Charlie Neucom, Ned Rush and family, Harry Boardman, Ed Schellbach and the Krause family. There were some very good players and often the club won district fixtures.

Walter Crowther (an uncle of the Krause boys) who lived at Imbil and was a very good player, once brought a group of Queensland champions up for a weekend of tennis – Emily and Bob Hood, Molly Pratten and Harold Wilson.

SWIMMING – A large deep swimming hole on the property.

FISHING – Excellent anywhere along the creek – cod, mullet.

EXPLORING THE SCRUBS

MEMORIES – TIMBER

Thirteen bullock teams and two horse teams used to operate past the farm. At one stage, the Council thought some of the culverts were unsafe for heavy loads and limited weights to 3500 super feet of timber. So, Christie Kropp loaded up with 4500 super feet of 'special' grade logs just to prove them wrong and made it safely through. You could always tell when he passed back empty from Imbil. There was a big gum tree at Andrew's Crossing, and he always cracked his whip once down the tree. It sounded like a gun going off.

Ned Rush was noted for drinking scalding hot tea. At dinner camps, when he came in sight, everyone made sure all the tea mugs were full before he got there. He could drink several mugs while the other men were sipping and waiting for the tea to cool.

Jimmy Ryan was another bullock driver and had a son about fourteen years old, both keen fishermen. They would often stake out as many as twenty to thirty lines in the creek. When asked once if they had done any fishing lately, the son replied, "We??? Haven't??? Got??? Any??? Time to??? Go to the ??? toilet."

Other teamsters were Joe Peterson, Henry Clark, Bill and Ted O'Leary, Ernie Wooster (a horse team). Three sawmills operated at Imbil – a State one, Luttons, and Meyers. Joe Peterson said the average man would eat a peck of dirt in a lifetime, but he, a bullock driver, would have eaten a bushel. (4 pecks = 1 bushel = 56 pounds = 25.4 kilograms).

MEMORIES – OTHER

Darky Friend was an Englishman who at one time had been a sailor. He lived past Boardman's towards the Dam just before the last crossing. He would go to Brisbane to see greyhound races. Monkeys at times rode on the dogs' backs. He thought they were very intelligent animals. "We've only lost our tails," he said.

People by the name of Saunders lived near Friends'. Mrs. Saunders was a French woman and Mr. Saunders a returned Digger.

Mrs. Rush (Ned's wife) had strong ideas regarding cleanliness. When the baker came, he was presented with a dish of water and a towel and made to wash his hands before handling her bread. When she bought chooks, she dosed them with Epsom Salts and no eggs were used until she felt sure they were clean inside. Ned used to say the poor chooks were "tucked up like curlews."

When ploughing a small paddock near Boardman's Crossing, Mr. Krause ploughed up a skeleton without a skull. It was thought to be an Aboriginal's, but nothing was ever proved about it.

L. Krause

Pigsty with shingle roof

PORTION 438, PARISH IMBIL, COUNTY LENNOX SHIRE WIDGEE

This farm was selected by Alec Andrews when Imbil Station was cut up for close settlement. The flats were heavily timbered with blue gum and native apple, while the ridge was timbered with ironbark. The creek banks had yielded their store of black bean and red cedar to the timber cutters decades before. Large amounts of silky oak were to be found in the creek area.

Alec cleared the flats and hill of most of the timber and established a dairy farm and grew corn and pumpkins successfully. His dairy herd consisted of Australian Illawarra Shorthorns, with I guess the occasional Hereford thrown in. He was a successful farmer and built a number of houses on the farm; the present farmhouse was built in 1924, and although altered from time to time is still basically the same.

When he retired to live in Brisbane, he built his home out of silky oak from the farm. A number of share farmers managed the property, with varying degrees of success, and the farm was sold to Bill Sanderson in 1947.

Bill only stayed for a year and in 1948 he sold the farm to Alf Priebe. The Priebe family have been there ever since. Alf wondered why Bill sold the farm and returned to the dryness of Monto. He also wondered what were the stumps of plants that covered the farm. He found his answer to both questions in spring the following year when the farm was covered with Noogoora Burr, which was battled constantly for the next thirty years.

The farm has always been a dairy and currently has 175 cows. The present owners are Rob and Pat Priebe; they have four children Sue 18, Steve 16, Mike 11 and Margaret 8.

ROBSON FAMILY

Tom and Mary Robson arrived in Imbil with their two children and a few possessions, all that remained of their worldly goods following the fire that destroyed their home in Gympie. Tom had been a miner and now, with the closing of the mines he was forced to take on whatever employment he could find. Jobs were non- existent in Gympie, so he took on a job with Alex Andrews as farm labourer and there was a small cottage provided and this too was an incentive.

Mary was in her early twenties, Tom some five years older, Tommy their son was a little over three and Beryl almost one year old. Tom Junior managed to keep himself and all concerned fully occupied; one heard tales of his exploits. On one occasion he thought he could do a better job than the sitting turkey and took up his position on the eggs. He couldn't understand how the turkey hen could cover the eggs without breaking them, as he was covered with the eggs. I don't think Mrs. Andrews was impressed.

On another occasion, his mother sent him with a billy- can to get the eggs and because the eggs were higher than the rim of the billy, he popped the lid on and sat on it. That problem was solved save for a few broken eggs. Nothing was sacred to that imp. One day he managed to get a bung out of the molasses keg – molasses everywhere – guess some kids are like that. However, all those problems were overlooked, and hearts melted in true country style the day Tom junior went missing. His mother thought he was with his dad and he in turn thought he had gone home to his mother. Panic reigned and a full-scale search was organised by the locals. The story has a happy ending. He was discovered at dusk with his dog on the hill behind Horne's property several miles away and on the opposite side of the creek.

Life was no bed of roses and the luxuries we have come to expect today as our rights were but a dream. Tom and Mary had few possessions. Their bed was ticking filled with corn husks. Their mode of transport a horse and sulky. On one occasion Beryl had a healthy crop of boils, one on her bottom preventing her sitting down. She was on her way into Gympie to see a doctor, but they arrived in Imbil just in time to see the train crossing the bridge. Five minutes late, they were filled with utter dismay.

Tom Senior and his co-worker mate Harold White would put the provisions in a wash tub and float it across the flooded creeks while they swam pushing it. The level crossings were frequently flooded, and the teamsters too would bring supplies to the farming folks. After a few years, the family moved to another place of employment where they had no flooded creeks. I have a sneaking feeling that whatever Tom's work was like, there would be those who would not shed a tear to see the back of junior. I never did hear how Mr. and Mrs. Andrews felt.

The Robson family lived on in Imbil and had four more children. The parents and eldest son (Tom) have now passed away.

Mary Freeman (nee Robson)

"ENROH" – YABBA CREEK

My father, Louis Horne, eldest son of James Horne of Monsildale Station, via Kilcoy, married Ella Vohland, eldest daughter of Peter Vohland, a farmer on the Darling Downs. Louis Horne and Ella Vohland were married in Toowoomba and came to Yabba Creek in 1915.

Imbil Station had been subdivided and Dad selected 190 acres on Yabba Creek. My parents named the property 'Enroh', which is Horne spelt backwards and pronounced N-RO.

They lived in a tent and cooked in a camp oven, while Dad felled the scrub, planted corn and fenced the property. He built a dip and stock yards. The dip was the only one on the creek in those days, and the dairy farmers and teamsters brought their cattle to be dipped. In the midst of all those early pioneering chores, Dad built a two-roomed dwelling, kitchen and bedroom. Later on, he added more rooms, verandas etc. This was to be our home for many years.

At a much later date, the old home was pulled down and a new one built. It is now occupied by Charles Simpson, who bought 'Enroh' from my brother Rae Horne who owned the property after Louis Horne passed on.

Louis Horne's father, James Horne, owned 'Borumbah' before my parents were married. Later on, I can't recall when, Borumbah became Dad's property.

Borumbah (we spelt it with an H added) was a lovely property, which included the Borumbah Creek.

My mother made many inquiries trying to find the meaning of the word Borumbah, and we think that Borumbah means high mountains.

I imagine it would be an aboriginal word.

Borumbah was ideally suited for cattle grazing. The cattle climbed the mountains for warmth during the winter and came down to the cool Borumbah Creek during the summer.

Dad sold Borumbah before the dam was built. The entrance is now covered with water.

We used 'Enroh' mainly as a holding paddock for our beef cattle, but during the Depression, we had a small dairy. My brother Rae used the property for dairying at a later date.

We had a happy life on 'Enroh', and I enjoyed riding to Borumbah with my father on odd occasions.

All those lovely little creek crossings and the bellbirds singing remains in my memory.

Jean Donald (nee Horne)

GEORGE GARRETT FAMILY
(1884-1967)

Born on his father's property at Moss Vale, New South Wales, George Garrett gained an early feeling for the land. Schooling was just long enough to enable him to learn to read and write. From an early age, he worked at labouring jobs including building roads, railway fettling (once called navvies), timber felling and snigging. He then started a carrying business in Dorrigo, New South Wales and owned several houses that he would rent. The last record, which I have, is payment that a Mrs. Mac dated 13.12.1915. Here he met and married Lila Elizabeth Smith.

By the end of the First World War, the desire to have his own property was strong. The decision to sell his business and houses was made. Retaining a few good pieces of furniture, kitchen necessities and packing the household linen and blankets in tin trunks, they loaded a horse-drawn wagon and headed for Queensland.

The intention was to buy a sugar farm, which he did, on the Maroochy River. The stay there wasn't very long as he wasn't very impressed with the swampy nature of the country and the ever-present swarms of mosquitoes.

On selling the Maroochy property, he bought an area of ground somewhere near Brooloo, but this still just wasn't what he was looking for.

At this time, Imbil Station had been cut into several blocks with two of the smaller blocks of ninety and seventy acres being considered to be the best farmland. One of these blocks on the Yabba Creek, now known as Foxes, was acquired by a Mr. Nicholls who later sold to

Bob Young (Mrs. T. Stubbins's father). On seeing this farm George approached Mr. Young who agreed to sell for the then fairly high sum of 4000 pounds. But it was good land, with approximately sixty acres of good alluvial flats and thirty-three acres of higher ground ideal for the farm buildings. This was about 1921.

At the time of settling on Yabba Creek, Nellie was a baby. There were two older children, Merle the eldest and Fred. Four more children were born over the next ten years.

Sylvia lives in Brisbane. Joel married and lived in Yass, New South Wales until his death in 1974. Daisy has remained in the area and lives in Gympie. Ivy, who was born in Imbil, still lives there. Nellie now lives in Bundaberg. Merle died in 1965 and Fred in 1969.

Mother Lila, died at a very young age in 1932. Merle, at the age of thirteen, was looking after the home with the assistance of Fred and a Mrs. Potter who came on wash days.

After the purchase of the property, there began many years of hard work to feed and clothe the growing family and to repay the bank loan. This George achieved mainly through growing maize. The ploughing, planting and scuffling were all done with horses, which he continued to use until he sold the property. The maize for planting was obtained by hand-shelling selected cobs. Only the middle grains of even shape and size were used, the remaining grain on the ends becoming feed for the animals. The task of shelling was done on wet days and all family members would do their share. The grain could be quite sharp and after a few hours, one's hands could become quite tender.

The maize crop had to be handpicked and stored in the barn which would almost be bulging at the sides, with cobs piled to the roof. Then the threshing began which was very noisy and dusty. At this time some labour had to be employed. The early threshing machine was a Massey Harris (one of a similar vintage can be seen in the back yard of the Imbil Hotel). This machine had to be hand-fed as each cob had to be rolled in sideways.

Later on, about 1933, a much bigger and faster machine, an Enterprise, was purchased. This machine was a big advancement as it was able to feed itself.

Time was all important to be able to produce three crops of maize in two years. The variety grown in those days was Yellow Dent which took six months to mature. The present-day varieties only four months.

Another reason for hurrying to get the crop off the paddocks was the fear the floods would cover the flats. (This did occur in 1955, several years after George had sold the property). Water did run through the crop and back up into the bottom area several times. The water-damaged grain together with cobs that birds had damaged and allowed weevils to enter was picked into separate heaps to keep for pig feed.

Pigs were a profitable sideline, a source of meat and home-cured bacon. Much of the meat had to be salted as ice chests were the only means of chilling food. Pigs were only killed in cooler weather as it was a hard meat to keep, even after the best of care of daily boiling and straining the brine to get rid of the blood.

Much of the grain was bagged and sent by rail to Brisbane markets. In the early days, it was taken by horse and wagon to the rail line and after 1930, J. Bath had a carrying business. With his truck, he could take several loads in one day.

Local storekeepers would buy a lot of the grain, but the forestry was the 'bread and butter' buyer as at that time all forestry work was done with horses. The horses were used for ploughing fire breaks and as pack animals. Even the forester and rangers had to have horses to be able to get to their area of work.

As the animals used for this type of work had to be very steady, young horses were sent to farmers to work. Many a young horse had its first taste of working life harnessed beside an old animal pulling a plough up and down those long furrows. Young horses were only worked a half day so there were usually two or three of them on the farm. The forestry would also let farmers use the horses in slack times to keep them in feed and good working condition.

Up until 1948, the forestry was still taking twenty bags of corn a month, but around then they dispensed with horses.

Once the bulk of the cobs had been threshed and sold, room became available for a dozen or more thousand-gallon water tanks in the barn. In these, a good portion of the grain was stored. This had to be really mature, dry grain or it would sweat and go mouldy. The purpose of this was to wait until other growers had sold their crop and the price would rise a little.

Farmers had their own methods of fumigating and sealing these tanks to prevent weevils attacking the grain. Once a tank was full, a small stub of candle in a tin was placed on top of the grain and lit. The tank then was closed and sealed. The candle would burn up the oxygen and go out. Frugal farmers would be able to use the same piece of candle several times. The area around the lid of the tanks and the bottom opening were covered with different homemade sealants – tar, flour, and soap being the chief ingredients in most of these. They worked – for on opening those tanks, up to twelve months later, the grain would be in perfect condition, with no sign of weevils. But leave the maize sit around in bags and the damage was enormous.

The growing of maize, with some small crops mainly for home consumption, remained the main source of profit until dairying commenced about 1939. Prior to this, four or five cows had been kept and looked after by the girls. Extra income was earned through the sale of home- made butter, milk and eggs.

No farm would have been complete without its twenty or more hens. The big black Orpingtons were favoured by many as good layers and were also a good table bird. Not like the white feather dusters we see running around today which are solely egg producers. Many a large hen and good rooster were sacrificed for the dinner table in times of flood, supplemented by jewfish caught in the receding water.

One local resident, who still lives in Imbil, would arrive on his motorbike and sidecar to buy produce. After a considerable time bargaining over price, he would leave, loaded with choice cabbage and cauliflower at tuppence (2c) each and big yellow Lisbon lemons at tuppence for a dozen.

The Second World War brought many changes. The two boys enlisted in the army but after twelve months the younger, Joe, was discharged underage as he was still only seventeen and a half. As farming was considered an essential service, he wasn't called again. Nellie and Sylvia also joined the forces. Merle had married.

A Bedford truck was purchased, making the trip to the railway station much quicker and we were able to attend the local picture show on Saturday night.

Prices for farm produce rose dramatically. The cream cheque alone, from the small herd of fifteen or twenty cows, being ample to live on. Still, some maize was grown. About this time an order was obtained for white corn (Hickory King), a large, grained maize for the making of cornflour. This order continued until the time of selling the farm.

Vegetables were in keen demand to feed the troops. Instead of bags of maize leaving the farm, it became bags of all types of vegetables.

Carrots were a major crop. Well I remember my first venture into earning my own pocket money. My sister, Daisy and I received threepence a hundred to wash them. If one were to send vegetables to the market these days topped, trimmed and in corn sacks, they would be dumped immediately.

One event that caused quite a furore during the war years was when a light plane in difficulties tried to land on the flats, then growing oats for the dairy cows. Unfortunately, the wheels clipped the fence which toppled the plane over. The pilot wasn't injured. The local home guard was called out to keep watch until Air Force personnel arrived from Kingaroy to dismantle the plane and load it onto trucks to take back to base. On writing to Fred, who at this time was in New Guinea, we included this piece of news. As you may have guessed, when he received the letter, all relevant details had been cut out.

The years after the war were comparatively easy as everyone seemed to have money, and prices for all farm commodities remained high. We had a couple of years with little rainfall but with ample stored water and feed they created no real problem.

With warnings from his doctors that the early years of hard work had taken their toll and as his heart was showing signs of strain, George put the property on the market. The sale was made about 1950.

He then retired to Noosa Heads for approximately two years but again felt the urge to farm. He bought a small fruit property at Amamoor, retaining this for a few years. After selling this place he finally retired to Brooloo and then to Gympie Hospital. He suffered a severe stroke and remained in hospital for seven years, dying in 1967 aged eighty-three R.I.P. Of George's descendants, there are four girls still living, thirteen grandchildren and nineteen great-grandchildren.

PORTION 34 PARISH IMBIL LIFE ON A DAIRY FARM AT BUTLER'S CORNER

From the years 1931-1935, during the 'Depression', there was a scarcity of work, and the timber mills were practically closed down. People were on relief funds. R.G. Stehbens, my father, leased the property of 200 acres (eighty-one hectares) at Butler's Corner from the Forestry Department. He bought a herd of cows and began dairying with me, Rob Stehbens, working the property on half shares. My sister Peg (now Mrs. Basil Blake) assisted me, and we lived in a shed, which was 15 feet x 10 feet.

Fifty-four cows were milked by hand in summer. There was fewer to milk in winter. I arose each day at 3 a.m. to begin milking which took three hours or more.

Round-up time in a hundred-acre (40.5 hectares) hilly, not fully cleared, paddock at 3 a.m. was difficult. I took the dog with me, rode the horse, and called out for the cows. Sometimes I would not see a cow until I arrived back at the bails. If when daylight came, there were any missing cows, I would have to go and find them.

The milk had to be separated by hand. The cream had to be transported by horse and sulky, four miles (6.5km) to Imbil Railway Station, to be sent at 7.30 a.m. by rail motor to Gympie butter factory. Milking began again at 3 p.m. Transporting the cream to the railway station in wet weather was a problem, as there were three Yabba Creek Crossings to drive through. There were no bridges on Yabba Creek in those days. One day, the water was high enough to float the cream cans out of the sulky and then they had to be held in. Another day, the horse stumbled, and its head went under the water. I had to jump out of the sulky and lead it through the swollen creek.

Butler's Corner is very susceptible to fog and some days it was impossible to locate some cows before 10 a.m. There was no refrigeration. If there was a flood in the creek the cream had to be held for three or four days so it was impossible to maintain A Grade Standard. But one year I obtained a Choice (A Grade) Certificate for the whole year's supply. At the butter factory, every can of cream sent in by the dairy farmers was graded by an official tester. It was this man's job to taste a sample of cream from each can and grade it accordingly.

Between milking times, the day was taken up with farming, growing mainly maize in summer and oats and wheat in winter.

Oat and wheat crops were grown as feed for cattle. Some vegetables including potatoes were grown and the amazing price of three pence (2 ½ cents) was the price obtained for large drumhead cabbages. Big-sized, long watermelons (30lb. weight – 13.5kg) were nine pence each (eight cents). First-grade butter fat was worth seven pence per pound (six cents). Pigs were worth three pence (2 cents) per pound, and they had to be between ninety pounds (41kg) and one hundred and twenty pounds (54.5kg) in weight. Anything weighing over or under this weight was paid less.

There was no market for calves. So, I had to kill, skin and boil them down to be used as pig feed. The skins had to be salted to send to market. This was to preserve them and keep them soft and the returned price was from two to four shillings (20 to 40 cents) per skin.

Corn (maize) was hand-picked and husked. It was shelled by a hand-powered sheller. Ploughing was done with a mould-board plough and two horses.

Bedtime was 8 p.m. One night, my partner called out that it must be time to get up as the willie wagtail birds were twittering loudly, it being a very moonlit night.

The main entertainment was a weekly dance in town which ended at 2 a.m. so by the time we drove back the four miles to the farm, it was time to round up the cows. Then when milking began and with our heads resting on the flanks of the cows, we were prone to 'doze off'. If the partner heard the flow of the milk in the bucket stop, the call was given to wake up.

There was no corner store handy. The day I ran out of sugar I substituted honey in my cup of tea. I found it a very unpleasant combination and it was ten years before I would enjoy eating honey again.

Another experience at milking time was the day a nearby tree was struck with lightning. To save time the cows were never chained up in the bails. On this occasion, I was left with a bucket of milk between my knees and no cow.

By 1935, the Depression had eased. I was glad to leave the farm for other employment. My father was able to purchase the Forestry house on the property where the share farmers who followed me lived.

Rob Stehbens

NEUCOM'S PROPERTY

In the early part of the century, our grandparents, John and Elizabeth Diggins, owned the Jones' Hill Hotel. For many years this was a popular overnight stopping-place for the Mary Valley people after delivering their pigs and produce to Gympie for sale.

In 1912, they sold the hotel and bought the property, 47V Parish of Imbil, from the Spiller family. They named the property 'Thistle Brae'. To this day, it is still owned by their daughter Jean English, who was one of the early teachers at the Provisional School at Imbil.

In 1918, our parents Charles Neucom and Caroline Diggins were married and settled on the adjoining property 46V, which had also belonged to Spillers. This property was named 'Rosedale' and has belonged to the Neucom family ever since. There were four children in our family, Viv, Bess, Doug and Len. In all kinds of weather, we walked or rode horses the three miles to school in Imbil. Bess and Viv doubled on one horse until Viv left school, then Doug replaced him.

Len, meanwhile 'hummed a doubler' whenever possible. Our cousins, the Tincknells, managed to load one horse up with three riders, Cyril, Mary and May, in that order. Other ponies were fortunate enough to have only two passengers. Our schooling was interrupted for many weeks at a time during the wet season owing to flooded crossings. Our dad rode across the flooded crossings with us when it was considered safe enough and we could continue our schooling.

There were times in the late 1920s when a few of us children, while walking to school, saw Aborigines walking along the creek bank a short distance from the road. Each respected the other and continued walking. Having told our parents, who seemed unconcerned, we realised that Aborigines also lived in this area. Doug and Len, the younger members of our family, continued to ride on horseback until Mr. Jim Ehrenberg ran his old truck to transport the children to school. In later years this service was replaced by a school bus.

In the early days, our father, Charles, owned a horse team and hauled timber to the sawmill in Imbil, owned by Mr. Les Doyle, and also the State mill. The team was used to cart corn from the neighbouring farms to the Imbil Railway. Later on, our dad went in for dairying and pig-raising.

We had an Illawarra dairy herd of 50-60 cows, which we milked by hand before and after school. My brother Len and I (the main milkers) would have milking contests. By memory, our best effort was thirteen cows in one hour, provided we had no interruptions from the cat, who would stand alongside with paws on our lap waiting for milk to be squirted into its mouth! There's nothing quite like – country fresh!

I can remember on one occasion when a family member was sick. Reverend Tom Sargeant, (the local minister), after conducting his service at Ridgewood, rode his pushbike back to Imbil and out to our farm. He stayed overnight and helped with the milking the following morning. He was a frequent visitor and often helped out with the family chores.

At first, the cream which was separated by hand, was taken to Kandanga by buggy by our mother. This was an all-day event, and the horses soon became aware of the frequent stops their drivers made to pass the time of day to any oncoming buggy. In fact, I'm sure that the horses came to enjoy the chit-chat even more than their drivers!

Later on, the railway line was continued to Imbil, so the cream was taken there, then on to the Gympie butter factory by train. Mr. Schellbach from up the creek, modernised things later on by transporting cream from farms along the creek by buckboard and then later, in his Buick.

Pigs were trucked to the sale yards at Brooloo by Dad, where they were sold by weight and held overnight, then railed to Brisbane the following day.

In conjunction with dairying, we grew corn, potatoes, pumpkins and lucerne. The soil was tilled by horse- drawn implements and the lucerne was cut and raked by a horse-drawn mower and rake. The hay was loaded onto a wagon by manpower and hay fork, and nesting magpies swooping down on us didn't make it a pleasant job!

Wagon load of hay

The corn crops were hand-picked and carted by wagon or dray and stored in the barn.

Fortunately, life was not all work, and fond memories are held of playing tennis at the 'White Rose' tennis court at Butler's Corner. I, Bess, did not make the 'A Grade' team as I was not built for speed and my racquet had more than the normal number of holes. Our jaunts out to the back paddock with the Tincknell gang were interesting. Our parents became uneasy when we had been away so long, but Uncle Alf knew the answer and he howled like a dingo. We were within earshot and took off at top speed. When we arrived home, Uncle Alf told us it was the biggest dingo he had ever seen – and we believed him! The grocery shopping was very different from today when the family car is driven to the local supermarket and the groceries are purchased on a regular basis. Mr. Henry Watson, employee of Mrs. Gilroy's store, would travel to the farms one day to collect orders and deliver them on the following day. The next week, Mr. Tom Afflick, employed by Moynehan's store, would do the same. The number of grocery items they could rattle off without a list was astounding.

People along the creek were cut off for long periods of time during floods, as there were no bridges. The late George Price (Snr) rescued many by bringing out supplies and then our dad and Uncle Alf would boat the cream over and bring back the supplies. At times a flying fox was used to deliver goods across the flooded creek.

The methods of transport steadily progressed. Timber trucks replaced the bullock and horse teams, and cream trucks took the place of horse and buckboard. Instead of droving cattle from point A to B on horseback, they were then taken by cattle trucks.

Modern inventions have certainly made everything faster but gone are the days when people had the time to chat over a good 'hot cuppa'.

We continued dairying until 1949 when the dairy herd was sold. During the same year, on October 5th, I, Bess Neucom, married Frederick Palmer and later on in 1951, our son, Lenard was born.

During the years 1949-1952, I, Len, the youngest son of Charles and Caroline Neucom, grew crops of maize and reared beef cattle on our property and the adjoining farm, 48V, which we leased from Mr. J Doyle.

Later the same year, I purchased a bulldozer and branched into the timber industry in conjunction with my two brothers, Viv and Doug. The standing timber was cut, snug and hauled to Lutton's Timber Mills at Imbil and Brooloo, the Imbil Railway Station and Wilson Harts' Sawmill at Kandanga.

We cut some really fine standing timber in the areas of Borumba, Bella Creek, Mudjimba and Ryan Creek where we camped on site from Monday until Saturday midday each week.

One particularly large red cedar log, felled in the Mudjimba area comes to mind. The butt log from this tree contained approximately 3500 super feet. It was cut at Lutton's Mill into boards 2½ inches thick and transported to South Australia for the manufacturing of fishing reels.

Red cedar log taken from the Borumba property, (left to right) Len Neucom and Charlie Neucom

On November 26th, 1955, I married Fay Patroni and built our home on the property alongside the existing family home. I continued with timber work for many years, meanwhile building up a dairy herd of 70-80 Illawarra and Jersey cattle.

Our son Greg, was born in 1958, followed by our daughter Glenda in 1960.

Dairying and pig raising along with the timber continued to be our livelihood, the milk being separated, and the cream transported to the Pomona butter factory. The separated milk was used to rear pigs and calves for future production. Some years later we dispensed with pigs and a refrigerated vat was installed and fresh milk was supplied to the Wide Bay Factory in Gympie. We continued working the farm in this way on a share basis until Mother passed away in 1966, when we took over full responsibility and ownership.

During the years 1969-1979, we began ginger growing, which gradually became our main source of income. We then relinquished our dairy herd and replaced them with Hereford beef cattle. We found the ginger a very interesting and exacting crop to grow, and the 10 acres grown each year provided casual work for large numbers of local people. The rhizomes were planted in August-September and grown under heavily irrigated conditions until the early harvest was picked in February-March. This was followed by another harvest in May and the late ginger being dug by potato diggers during winter.

The ginger was transported to the Buderim Ginger Factory in large wooden bins where it was processed. While preparing land for ginger growing, we uncovered many Aboriginal artifacts, including stone axes and spearheads which have since become collectors' items.

In the late 1970s, our 400 kiwifruit vines and 100 avocado trees were also planted. As kiwifruit is a vine of strong, climbing nature, trellises and pergolas had to be erected and windbreaks surrounding the blocks were planted. Several varieties of female vines were chosen with male pollinators planted at regular intervals.

As it would be some years before these crops became productive, we grew a wide variety of vegetables and strawberries. As a selling outlet for these and other local produce, we built a weekend roadside stall on our property fronting Yabba Creek Road, which we operated for the next nine years.

Two years ago, when our kiwifruit and avocadoes became viable, we installed a fruit grading machine, which handles both crops effectively. The fruit is packed and sent by road transport to the southern markets.

Presently we are kept busy with our current crops and cattle.

Over the years we have seen many changes in properties, farming techniques and lifestyles, but, to us, farming is still a peaceful and rewarding way of life.

Neucoms

Charlie Neucom ploughing

PORTION 100V – PARISH BROOLOO

We first came to Imbil about 1916 when we lived in a hut at Neucom's Crossing. While living there, Mum used to take us for a swim nearly every day in summer which we enjoyed greatly. It wasn't free of danger, what with snakes, scrub ticks etc to be concerned about, nevertheless it was one of the highlights of living there.

A few years later, Dad bought the property adjoining the reserve, from the Rowlands family. On this property, there was a house mainly built of slabs with a long kitchen at the back separate from the building where Mum did her washing. In those days it was boiling the clothes in a copper, for which we had to chop the wood.

Dad owned a bullock team which he used to haul logs from up the creek to the sawmill and railway log yard for many years until trucks took the place of bullock teams.

Quite a few men owned their own teams. One of the highlights we remember well is how they would all pull up at our gate for a drink of billy tea. When Dad arrived at Neucom's Crossing, he would crack the whip. Then Doris or I would get busy and make this large billy of tea.

Ted, the eldest in our family, Doris, and I would walk the two miles to school and really enjoy it until one day we were on our way to school when we heard the sound of hooves coming. Next, we heard a shout from the butcher who was droving the cattle to the slaughter yards.

"Look out, they will charge." We were so scared we went through the barbed wire fence into the forestry paddock and climbed trees. Needless to say, by this time one of the bullocks was through the fence in the same paddock. A lucky escape!

Harold was five years younger than me and by the time he was ready for school, we took a shortcut through the Mill yard. There were so many bindi eyes (prickles) that the men nick-named Harold "Bindy".

Later the boys rode to school on their horses, but Doris and I still walked, getting a ride sometimes in a vehicle if we were lucky.

By this time, Dad had put enough money aside to get a house built by the Swizler brothers.

When the boys left school, they ploughed quite a few acres and planted crops of maize, pumpkin, arrowroot etc. They would then plant a crop of cow peas to plough back into the ground to return the nitrogen to the soil.

Dad bought some cows later on and built bails and yards. Mum, Doris, and I milked up to thirty-two cows by hand morning and night, then turned a separator by hand to separate the cream. That wasn't the last of the cream. We used to harness a horse and take the cream to the railway station in the sulky.

E. Wallader

PORTION 25V – PARISH IMBIL

Christian Kropp bought a farm about one mile from Imbil on the right-hand side of Kropps Crossing, which was named after our family. He had a bullock team and hauled timber from the upper reaches of Yabba Creek.

His wife, Wilhelminnie, and the nine children, four boys and five girls, milked the cows and grew corn, potatoes, pumpkins and other small crops. The ground was cultivated with two draught horses and a twelve-inch hand plough. The cream was taken to the railway station by horse and sulky and sometimes on the pummel of the saddle. Fresh milk from this property was sold to the residents of Imbil. The children carried the milk by hand in billy cans to the householders on their way to school. The price for milk was 3 pence a pint. The school was on the Imbil Station, and they had to walk another mile to school after delivering the milk.

When the creek was in flood, the milk and children were transported across the creek by rowing boat. One evening as Christie was going across the flooded creek, who should wander along but me. I was four years old at the time. Christie sat me at the back of the boat and as we all know, accidents do happen and as the boat was pushed out into the flooded creek, it hit a snag and I fell out. I was told later that he jumped into the boat, put his hands over the back and caught me by the tips of my fingers. Events make impressions on your mind, and I will never forget that one.

My oldest brother, Willie used to help drive the bullock team consisting of twenty to twenty-four bullocks bringing mostly pine logs to the three mills and the railway yard. The average load of timber hauled by the bullocks was between 3000 to 4000 super feet. The railway truck wagons held 4000 to 5000 super feet and the timber was railed to different places all over the country.

Christie sold the farm seven years later and bought land in the township of Imbil. A house was bought in Gympie, dismantled and rebuilt on the site. The family continued milking and delivering fresh milk to the townsfolk. This ceased in 1974 when Victor, a brother, passed away. After writing this article, I realised that the Kropp family sold fresh milk to the people of Imbil for just on sixty years.

Alf Kropp

A wagon load of pine being hauled to the sawmill in Imbil. Christian Kropp standing beside wagon; son Willie on top of the logs.

MRS. M DWYER RECOLLECTS

It was a big project for Imbil when the dam was being built. Our men folk did the cutting and clearing of timber from the dam site.

Olly, my husband, had contracts to haul out the timber to the mills. I used to take the children to spend the day and picnic in the bush. I always think of a lovely rocky gully above the dam site with beautiful ferns and staghorns of all sizes on the rocks. It must have been covered by the dam.

In later times, Olly bought a farm with no fences, lots of rubbish and tangled wire. He made it into a dairy farm. He did a lot of work in a little time, and we all had work too. We had a lot of ups and downs.

We started off building a temporary yard and bails on the creek bank. My daughter-in-law and I had to travel out from town to milk the cows. In wet weather, it got very boggy.

Olly went to Cooroy and bought twenty very poor cows. On the first afternoon, we had to yard them, they knocked down our temporary yard. Did we have a picnic! They ended up a very good line of cattle when they picked up.

The biggest tragedy of all was the 1973 flood when we lost forty head of cattle. Olly wasn't there to see it. I was thankful for that much.

REX TWEED REMEMBERS

Wallader's blacksmith shop where many gathered to talk.

Old lady Price and Constable Galligan who saw every train in and out of Imbil.

Moynehan's old shop.

Mrs. Pestorious who ran the school when the principal went to the war.

LIFE ON YABBA CREEK FARM MID-TWENTIES TO FORTIES

We had to make our own entertainment – there being no tractors, horses were used for farming. This made it easy for us to play farming. Dragging trace chains through the grass with the hook catching the grass so it was piled up for hay was a favourite pastime. We were driven as horses with rope reins, one to each chain. It was hard going. When we had the pile as high as our knees, that was our stack. Or we were harnessed to a box which was filled with bits of wood. This was firewood, as there was no electricity.

The pet situation was plentiful – chickens, cats, dogs, possums, lizards, pigs and butterflies. These were our playthings.

One of our pet pigs was reared on our bitch who happened to have pups at the time – she made a good mother. It was also hand-fed on cow's milk.

One of our favourite games was races. Our kittens were good subjects. One kid would hold the mother while the other kids took three kittens a short distance and let them go. First to reach Mum was the winner. Also worm, cop this lot! In wet weather, we used to get worms and tie them in a single knot. First one out straight won. The shouting that went on was deafening.

We used to play house. Our cubby was inside lantana that grew up into a fig tree. We built shelves in the branches.

We started helping with work from seven to eight years old, doing jobs suitable for our age. This was in the Depression years. We could ride horses of course. We learned to milk cows by hand, feed calves, pigs, chooks and help pick up potatoes. This was for kids under ten years old. For kids over that age, it was pick corn, help unload the wagon and load cobs into the thrasher on thrashing day. Of course, getting cows was an everyday chore from when quite young.

The Bella Junction School opened and was quite a help for us up the top end. One thing we did was get out of the schoolyard, which we weren't supposed to do, to go exploring down the creek. Of course, we didn't hear the school bell! The teacher would have to come and find us. We only did it a couple of times as we ended up being caned so that stopped.

Our breaking-up day was a real picnic. All mums and dads came. We had games and races with boiled lollies as prizes.

The bullock wagons used for timber carting were one way of getting a ride to school at Bella School. We could hear them coming a mile away, so it was hurry up to get a ride. We would leave them at the Deep Crossing and run up the road to school, usually a bit late but being so hot Teacher couldn't say anything.

When we went to Imbil School, after Bella closed down, it was a different matter. We were driven to school in the sulky, four sitting on the seat and one on the floor.

By this time there were some timber trucks on the road, so care had to be taken. One big one had iron wheels with solid rubber tyres and used to pull such a load up the hill that when changing gears, the engine would buck up and the front wheels would lift off the road.

It was just over an hour to get to school. One of our habits was carving names on trees. The boys used to do this with pocket knives.

During the wet season, it was quite usual for one of the people up the creek to ring the party line to say the creek was rising. We would know it was on, as about one or two o'clock, the headmaster would come and say, "All creek kids, children, go home."

So, it was out and on the horses, and full belt through town with about sixteen horses galloping with shouting kids. It must have been a warning to town people that the creek was rising. Dad would be at our last crossing to see us safely across as it was deep and dangerous, with swirling water halfway up to one's knees while sitting on a horse. Dad usually rode a draught horse to get us over and was on the top side, so he broke the force of the stream. We thought it was quite a thrill.

To get supplies of food when creeks were up, meant a long trip on horses, with packs around Western Creek. When the men were trying to get home after droving cattle to Pomona, and crossings were a swim for horses, it was a case of slip off the horse's back and hang on to the tail. Bert Atthow used to do this. He was rather brave, as not being a strong swimmer, he would cross flooded creeks in a dray which was all but floating.

Ted Schellbach had the cream run in a buckboard and four horses. He ran it three times a week. He brought supplies back at midday.

The White Rose tennis courts were started in the twenties. We were the ball collectors as small kids and played tennis as we grew up. Just before the war we played tennis every Sunday and had wonderful days. In those days, and when war broke out, we used to go dancing on Saturday nights until about two or three in the morning, have a couple of hours sleep, get up, milk cows by hand, play tennis all day, come home, (a walk which was one and a half miles) and milk again.

By then we were ready for bed. Next day – well, we won't go into that!

To smooth the court, Ray Atthow used to hook an iron wagon wheel on to the A Model Ford and drag it around the court. Anyone who watched this process went home rather dusty.

Imbil show was on about the end of corn picking time, so if the last patch of ten acres of corn was picked, we were taken for two days to the show.

When war broke out, young people started to drift away to war and to get married. Those years were hard, as things were difficult to get and we had to mend equipment, fences, roofing, etc., with what we could. Girls had to help out with farming. Horses were still used, as petrol was short, even for tractors, and power kero was used for most engines.

G. & M. Nicholson (Boardman)

LIFE ON A FARM

The farm was a peaceful place to live and work with good neighbours. We worked from daylight to after dark, milked cows twice a day, cleared the land of rubbish and worked the crops.

Saturday night, however, was set aside for the pictures, a dance or a visit to friends. Our local dances were the thing of the day. Brooloo, Imbil and Kandanga were the main hunting places. Brooloo seemed to be the pick. After the dance, we'd go home for a few hours sleep and then be up to milk.

After the war was settled, there were lots of young people about. A tennis court was started at the top of Friend's Crossing, but being young families with babies arriving, things came to a stop. We had some good picnics. Tewantin and Noosa were our spots for the beach and holidays. Our visits were few and far between.

In the wet season from January to March, we would have one flood after another. Sometimes we would be isolated for ten days at a time. The biggest flood was in 1951. It had been raining all day and we made an early start at the milking. From the back door, looking at the creek, we saw the roots of a tall oak and then the top would come up. Next thing the gully below the bails was full of water. There had been a cloud burst at Kingaham Creek and a wall of water was causing the damage. This was before the dam.

The Rodgers family came to inspect the farm just after the flood and had to walk from Andrew's Crossing where they left their car. They ended up buying the place.

The things you do! The creek was in flood and the spider bridge was covered but we could still see it. I tried to cross the creek with the cream in our truck. Our side of the bridge was in some still water, so I got through that but in the centre of the bridge, the rush of water picked up the front of the truck and put the wheels over the side. The Neucom boys came up with a team and pulled the truck out the next day. So I got the cream across the slow way – walked!

After the rain, our three eldest and the dogs would go into the gully and play. On this day they made a place where they could slide down the bank. This was good fun with plenty of laughter. They came home covered in mud from head to toe. May was happy as you can guess.

We employed people at times. We had some interesting ones including a New South Wales league footballer and a Dutch lad. The Dutch lad wanted to have two baths a day before meals. He would always stop work a half to three-quarters of an hour before meals so he could bath and dress to eat. He was soon told he was in the country. Because he had travelled, he was interesting to listen to. Another interesting worker was a middle-aged man who was quite a reader. His room was on the open veranda with roller canvas blinds. After he left, we saw on the inside of the blind a beautiful picture of the mountains about the house drawn in coloured chalks. It must have been his hobby along with books. The things you don't know about people.

With all the hard work, we enjoyed making our fun by taking the young children out with us on a slide and horses to do some clearing up in the paddocks. We would have a picnic and boil the billy. May always left the sugar at home which broke us off using sugar.

We pulled clumps of lantana with two horses – pulling one way and then the other, breaking off the roots. Lots of equipment got broken.

While the creek was dirty after a flood, we went fishing and made a picnic of it. When the water was clean, we'd go at night. Some big fish came from the hole. We always seemed to get some. Those were the good old days.

Gwen Boardman standing beside a 22lb cod caught in Yabba Creek

QLD COUNTRY LIFE, OCTOBER 6, 1983

This wild deer was too smart

OUR working bullocks at one time grazed "up the Borgan" – a beautiful valley some miles west of Imbil, with bellbirds and currajongs delighting our ears.

It was thickly wooded in parts, and didn't these bullocks love to lurk in any wooded gully when it was mustering time – they stood motionless to avoid sounding their bells.

Laddie, the good dog that he was, winkled them out from their hiding places and brought them in, with the musical bells swinging and ringing lustily.

One winter day, among the muster was a deer – a young stag with quite a fine pair of antlers. To Father's surprise, he stayed with the bullocks right into the yard and was still there while yoking up proceeded. The deer did not seem unduly timid and seemed to watch proceedings with interest.

As the team moved out, he easily and gracefully slipped over the six-foot high railings in one fluid movement. My husband thought it merely a one-time incident and gave it little thought but the next day, the same thing happened, and so on for many days.

After several days, Father gently tried to put his hand on it but no, that was too much, and over the rail like a flash went the graceful creature.

One of my husband's brothers was with us for a while and was so intrigued by this deer he concocted a crazy idea.

With saplings, he raised the height of the yard to prevent this wild beauty's daily escape, but to his chagrin, the resourceful animal flattened itself to the extent, antlers and all, it slipped under the rails – not much higher than a foot from the ground. The deer let a day or two elapse before returning but return it did, unaware that this crazy young man was building a sleigh on small wheels preparatory to catching the deer, taming the wild creature to pull this sleigh through the township during the approaching Christmas season.

He blocked up the lower rails of the yard and felt all was set – no animal, even a deer, could escape either over or under that yard.

Father looked on mildly amused, knowing full well the odds were in favour of the deer. Try as he would, using every ruse in his power against the deer which seemed almost as if enjoying the game of wits, brother could not outsmart that deer, which soon after must have heard the true call of the wild for it disappeared.

We often wondered if it became bored with this one- sided clash of wits and vanished to his own kind where at least intelligence would be more evenly balanced.

So Santa Claus still drives his sleigh unchallenged.

Mrs. F.M. Burke

REMINISCENCE

My personal memories of my early years on the farm are happy – I loved the freedom, the lovely blue hills, the trees, birds and wildflowers. Not having the company of children my own age didn't worry me. There were always ponies to ride, dogs to throw balls for and calves to be caught and fed. Sticks were wrapped in pretty colours to become people, houses were made out of wooden pegs, cars were old shoes and corn cobs and horseshoes became farm animals.

The yearly floods would leave great banks of clean sand and I remember sliding down these and getting my clothes filthy. We swam in Yabba Creek with its beautiful clear, clean water before the building of the dam and heavy irrigation. Many an exciting race was held in the shallow but quickly flowing water using bean pods as boats. On tiring of this, we sank the boats by bombarding them with rocks. Small fish were caught by dropping rocks on them, to be released later and we felt sad if they didn't respond and swim away.

On Guy Fawkes night, the older family members let off the skyrockets which never did come up to expectations.

Nights were spent sitting at the lamplit table helping to prepare the fruit and vegetables for the jams and pickles that were made in huge quantities. They had to last the year, as there was no going to the corner shop to replenish supplies. I remember the mouth-watering smell of biscuits and cakes baking made from home- produced milk, butter and eggs. This was almost a daily chore. Hens were usually allowed to roam free, so younger children were given the task of finding the nests before the crows and goannas.

I remember watching the oats fall before the sweep of the scythe, sadness at finding a bird's nest in the path of the workers, helping to pile the hay on the horse-drawn wagon until it was so high only the men could throw the hay to the top, riding back to the barn on top of the sweet-smelling hay, feeling a bit nervous about being so high but loving every minute of the trip.

Days were spent following the plough to catch mice to keep as pets, but mysteriously the mice always seemed to get out at night. At the end of the day, we were placed on the back of a large draught horse for the walk back to the barn where the horses were scrubbed down, watered and fed great nose bags of fresh chaff and corn.

The arrival of the yearly catalogues from McDonnell & East, Finney Isles and others, was eagerly awaited. From these, nearly all the yearly necessities would be ordered. Going through the catalogue after the elders had finished with them, we wondered did anyone buy the toys that were pictured. The arrival of the huge cardboard cartons caused great excitement as each was opened to reveal the paper-wrapped parcels in a bed of wood shavings. Then all would be revealed – a lovely milk jug, cups and saucers, rolls of flannelette to be made into shirts, which all farmers seemed to wear, unbleached sheets which had to be washed and hung out wet for several days and dewy nights until they became sparkling white and soft, tea towels, bath towels and sometimes something special such as a lovely flower vase.

School days mark the end of a magic time of make- believe and the beginning of growing up. I was fortunate, as my school days began a little late, as I had to ride double bank with my sister and so was given an extra year to grow a bit bigger.

The creek seemed to flood every year and a lot more schooling was missed. In all those days, riding to school through wet seasons and summer storms, the only time I got really wet, was whilst in the company of several other girls as we sat in Kropps Crossing.

On arrival at school, we reported to the teacher that we were wet, and we were allowed to return home which took us all morning. We had a lovely time talking, eating our lunches, and stopping at Neucom's Crossing to gather raspberries. We checked to see if the finger cherries were ripe.

We would meet quite a few interesting people on our journey to and from school – the road gang with their horse and cart – Julius Hartvigsen and wife, Minnie, on their way by sulky to work their plot of ground at Butler's Corner and bullock wagons, although trucks were fast taking over.

One other event caused quite a stir. This concerns my brother and several other boys who used to wag school occasionally. Smoking seemed to have been their chief form of entertainment, but on this day, they decided to put flank ropes on the ponies. I don't know how the other boys fared, but my brother had to be taken to hospital for a short stay having put a tooth through his bottom lip and suffering several other cuts and bruises. I think that put an end to group wagging, but individual boys would still be mysteriously absent.

If girls ever wagged school, I didn't know about it, but years later, when the school bus had started, I did deliberately miss that on a few occasions. This would still be practised today which shows that with all the changes that have taken place, people remain very much the same.

MEMORIES - FIRST PLANE

We were at the show grounds on Imbil Show Day. Suddenly, our dad pointed up to the sky at what we children thought was a bird.

Dad said, "See that thing up there? That is an aeroplane and there is a man inside it."

I remember thinking that Dad was having a joke with us! Of course, that was the first plane I had ever seen. As the planes in those days were very small, and it was flying high, I still remember it as looking exactly like a bird.

Jean Donald (nee Horne)

PLEASURES AND PERILS OF SCHOOL DAYS

We, as children of Yabba Creek, went to school in Imbil and like all children, we got up to pranks.

I recall tormenting a snake when a teamster came along and rescued us and killed a DEATH ADDER! We thought we were trying to kill a lizard!

Another day, we got off our horses and tried to kill what we thought was a death adder. We were tormenting it with sticks when it got fed up and spread out its frill. It was a frilled lizard!

At Neucom's Crossing after rain, there was a clay cutting through the bank at the side of the road, which became very slippery. We used to amuse ourselves by riding our horses down this slippery slope. It was so slippery our horses had to skate down. I shudder to think what would have happened if a horse had fallen.

After going to a circus, we spent lots of time on the way to and from school trying to copy the circus performers. We used to ride our horses sitting backwards. We would stand up in our saddles and put our horses to a trot and finally (after much practice) to a canter. If we felt we were losing our balance, we promptly spread our legs and flopped back into the saddle.

One of the most dangerous escapades was when we swam our horses backwards and forwards across what was then called the Deep Hole at Neucom's Crossing. At that time none of us could swim!! Our parents would have been horrified.

A tribe of Gypsies camped at Kropps Crossing for a while. We were fascinated by their bright clothing, large earrings, head scarves and their dark complexions, and flashing dark eyes. I can't recall how long they camped at Kropps Crossing, but we were disappointed when they left. They were the only Gypsies I have ever seen.

The eight Horne children on horseback ready for school

MEMORIES - FIRST CAR

My early memories of our transport are a buggy drawn by two grey mares called Bess and Jess.

I was aged about 2 1/2 and my brother Evan 13 months younger, when we experienced a remarkable event, which is very clear in my memory to this day.

I had never set eyes on a car – hadn't heard the word car, when one day Evan came to me with his eyes almost popping out of his head, and said, "Jeanie, look, look!! What's that?!"

We ran out onto our eastern veranda and there was this strange 'thing' coming along the road without horses pulling it. We watched fascinated! The 'thing' came up the hill, and turned towards our place, so we rushed on to our northern veranda. Then the 'thing' passed our dip and yards and pulled up at our gate and wonder of wonders, our dad stepped out. That day, I shall never forget.

When I see all the traffic on the roads today, my thoughts sometimes go back to that remarkable day when Dad stepped out of that T Model Ford.

Actually, our car was the first car on Yabba Creek; and sometimes Dad conveyed people towards Gympie to meet the ambulance. One day, a baby was born in the back of the car, on the way to meet the ambulance.

Fortunately, Dad had taken Imbil's midwife with him. Mother and babe both survived and continued on to meet the ambulance.

Jack and Jean Donald with daughter

MEMORIES - FIRST WIRELESS

One afternoon we were riding home from school, when Mr. Tarry, who lived across the road from Lutton's Mill, came up to us and asked if we would like to hear a voice from many miles away.

We tethered our horses and went into Mr. Tarry's place. Mr. Tarry placed earphones on our ears, and we all took turns to listen to "the voice from many miles away." We were fascinated, and hurried home to tell our parents of this miracle.

Mr. Tarry was the first person in Imbil to get a radio (or wireless as it was called in those days).

Jean Donald (nee Horne)

MEMORIES - THE GOLDEN SOVEREIGNS

My father once sold a horse for £8 to a man who lived a nomadic lifestyle and appeared in Imbil on rare occasions. Nobody knew where he lived, and I can't recall his name.

The day he took delivery of the horse, he told Dad he didn't have the money on him, but he would pay for the horse sometime in the future.

Months went by. Dad said, "I think I may as well say goodbye to that £8."

A few more months passed, and Dad came home from Imbil saying he had been paid for the horse. He rolled eight beautiful golden sovereigns across the table! The sovereigns had been handed in to the banks years before – I had never set eyes on a sovereign.

Dad said, "I wonder how many more he has hidden away?"

Some of those early prospectors were distrustful of banks and hid their sovereigns. As some of these old men gradually passed on, the secrets of their hiding places died with them. I believe there could be large fortunes of golden sovereigns still hidden beneath the earth.

Jean Donald (nee Horne)

MEMORIES - "BLACK WHISKERS" OR "THE HAIRY MAN"

Some people called him "Black Whiskers", and some called him "The Hairy Man," but he carried his 'Bluey' and appeared in Imbil on rare occasions during the early 1920s.

He had long black hair and whiskers, which reached to his waist. He was quite harmless, but rather scary in appearance.

Nobody knew his name or where he came from. There came a time when he just didn't appear anymore, so it is unknown to this day what became of him.

One afternoon as we were riding home from school, "Black Whiskers" was resting by the roadside at Kropps Crossing.

We never saw him again.

Jean Donald (nee Horne)

LOVELY – OUR PET DEER

Living in the country, we were always surrounded by animals. At different times we had special pets from the dog, cat, cattle, and sheep families. For a while, we had a pet kangaroo, but the most interesting pet was a female deer we called Lovely.

One day, Dad was riding along on one of our grazing properties when suddenly, he came across a newborn deer. The mother deer galloped away, and Dad, with the help of his cattle dog, managed to capture the fawn and of course, brought her home.

Moya Horne feeding "Lovely"

We tethered her beneath the house. For a while, she was so wild and untamed, she would strike us with her front feet if we dared to go too close to her. We had to place her food on a flat dish, take a long stick, and push the food to within her reach. Gradually, Lovely realised we weren't going to hurt her. She became so protective towards us it was quite touching. We led her around for a long time then she progressed to galloping around the house yard. Finally, she had her freedom to roam the paddocks and chum up with the cattle and sheep.

Lovely could be mischievous on occasions, especially on washing days, as like a goat, she loved to chew clothing. Washing day became quite a ritual. We had to close her in the stockyard before we dared hang out the washing. On those days, she became quite cunning, and it often took a while to entice her to the stockyard. Lovely was very fond of sweets, so we usually coaxed her to the yard by holding a few lollies in our hand. It took ages to get her to take that final step so that we could close the gate.

One day, my sister washed out three pairs of stockings and hung them on a line beneath the house. That night, the last member of the family to come through to the house yard forgot to close the gate. The next morning, six stocking tops were all that was left on the line! I marvelled at how Lovely could digest all that fabric.

Once, we had a visitor who parked his car in front of our house and left the car door open. We were inside talking and having a cup of tea when one of the family walked out onto the veranda. There was Lovely, chewing a feather filled cushion which had been on the front seat of the car. The feathers were floating everywhere like snowflakes falling, while Lovely calmly chewed away at the cushion cover.

Lovely could be a trial at times when she chewed clothing, but she was quite loveable, like her name, when she showed protectiveness towards us. She would not allow a strange dog to come close to our house. On one occasion, visitors arrived at our place about midmorning and stayed until late afternoon. The visitors brought a dog with them and Lovely spent all day placing herself exactly between the dog and the house. If the dog shifted, Lovely promptly shifted too. She didn't eat or drink all day until the visitors left.

Henry Benson, a friend of my parents, decided to leave Australia and migrate to Kenya in Africa. He called in to say goodbye and Mum happened to be outside washing. When Henry put out his hand to shake hands with Mum, Lovely laid her ears back and promptly struck Henry in the chest.

I'll always remember the beauty of Lovely as she galloped so fleet footedly around the paddocks. Most of all, I'll never forget her protectiveness towards us all.

Jean Donald (nee Horne)

With Lovely, the deer

QUEENSLAND WATER RESOURCES COMMISSION BORUMBA DAM

The saying goes that you can't stop progress and in 1960, a site was selected to build a dam on Yabba Creek. The dam was called Borumba, and the structure was completed in 1964. Its purpose is to provide an assured supply of water for irrigation by private pumping from Yabba Creek and the Mary River for the Pie Creek Diversion Scheme, the Lower Mary Irrigation Project, and town water supplies such as the town of Imbil, the city of Gympie, the Noosa District and Maryborough. The storage area is also used for recreation such as water skiing, fishing, sailing, and canoeing. An area of land below the wall has been landscaped and picnic facilities are provided for the public.

Borumba Dam under construction

WELCOME TO LAKE BORUMBA FISH HATCHERY

Thank you for calling at our fish display building. The majority of the fish specimens on display are found in the Mary River system with the exception of the Australian Bass and the European Carp.

The Australian Bass is found in coastal streams usually in the fresh or brackish water from the Noosa River and Tin Can Bay areas in the north, to the Gippsland area (Victoria) in the south.

The European Carp is to be found at this stage, in the Murray Darling River System and currently extending to the St. George area in Queensland.

The Hatchery was established by the Queensland State Government in 1980/81 and transferred to the Widgee Shire Council in January 1986.

The Hatchery breeding programme includes Golden Perch (commonly known as Yellow Belly) and Silver Perch (or Black Bream) with emphasis on production of Golden Perch fingerlings for release into public waters.

The brood stock is collected from western areas during the winter months and transferred to the Hatchery in a 1000-litre tank. Once back at the hatchery, the fish are quarantined and subsequently placed in the large concrete holding ponds, until immediately prior to the breeding season, which usually commences during October.

When the water temperatures are suitable, the male and female broodstock are selected and injected with a hormone, then placed in a breeding tank.

When the larvae (newly hatched fish) are five days old, they are transferred into growing-out ponds. At approximately forty days old, the fingerlings are removed from the growing out ponds and treated for parasites prior to being transferred into plastic bags or suitable containers for transport to their ultimate destination. Fingerlings have been released into the Mary River and other public waters in the area, in a stocking programme that will ultimately improve the quality of recreational angling in the area.

At the end of the breeding season, the broodstock is measured, weighed, tagged, the number recorded, and the fish are released.

BRISBANE GIRLS GRAMMAR SCHOOL

On August 9, 1987, the Brisbane Girls' Grammar School Memorial Outdoor Education Centre officially opened. The Centre was established as a permanent memorial to two teachers and two former students, all of whom lost their lives in a bus accident in 1979. It is an annex to the Brisbane Girls' Grammar School and all funding for buildings, equipment, wages, and maintenance originates from the school.

The Centre is run by two qualified teachers. Sue Lanham and Tim Lanham. Sue is a science teacher and Tim is a physical education teacher. Much of the work at the Centre is non-teaching and involves food preparation, ground maintenance, and general repair. Girls visit the Centre on at least three occasions during their secondary schooling. Year 8 and Year 10 camps are of seven days duration and Year 9 for five days.

During their stay in the Valley, girls are introduced to a variety of activities such as rock climbing, abseiling, canoeing, camping, bushwalking and navigation. They also study various aspects of the local area. It is emphasised that the outdoor Education Centre is not a 'holiday camp' and indeed much of the girls' time is spent away from the Centre. The programme aims to develop the girls' initiative, self-reliance, self-esteem, and comradeship throughout the three years.

In Year 10, the students undertake a four-day expedition that involves a variety of skills that have been learned during prior visits to the Centre. During the expedition, groups must navigate their way across the backcountry from Mr. Allan's to the Centre via Summer Creek, Little Yabba Creek, Borumba Creek, Borumba fire tower, and canoe down the dam to finish. During this time the girls carry all their own food and necessary camping gear in backpacks and must do without the usual comforts of home. The prospect of hot showers and a sit-down meal at the Centre provide a suitable incentive for the groups to successfully complete the expedition.

At this stage, the Centre is visited only by Girls' Grammar students. However, use can be made of the Centre and its facilities by local school groups and organisations at times when the complex is not occupied by Girls' Grammar students.

Saddles ready to go at the Borgan

www.ingramcontent.com/pod-product-compliance
Lightning Source LLC
Chambersburg PA
CBHW062050290426
44109CB00027B/2783